Teaching Playskills to Children with Autistic Spectrum Disorder:
A Practical Guide

By

Melinda J. Smith M.D.

Editor: Linda Julian, Ph.D.
Book Design: John Eng
Cover Art: Ramon Gil

Library of Congress Control Number: 2001094242
ISBN Number: 0-9665266-3-5

Printed in the United States of America

*Dedicated to
my sons*

Acknowledgements

I wish to thank the parents and professionals of the ME-list for sharing with me their extensive knowledge, support, stories, encouragement, dedication, humor, and common sense. I could not have run my home ABA program or helped my child without them.

I also want to thank the contributors to my website for taking the time to make their experiences and advice available to parents worldwide. My 1999 website "Teaching Playskills to Children with Autism" (http://melindasmith.home.mindspring.com) formed the impetus for creating this book.

I want to thank my older son for tolerating the extreme attention paid to his younger brother, for growing into such a strong, creative, and brilliant young man, and for loving his brother "no matter what."

I want to thank my younger son for teaching me patience, for showing me a world viewed through different eyes, and for demonstrating the joy of simple pleasures.

I also want to thank my editor Linda Julian, Ph.D., for her encouragement, for her patient grammar instruction, and for her ability to improve my writing style to make it more closely resemble that of an adult.

Table of Contents

Chapter 1: Teaching Playskills 1
Definitions of Play 2
The Development of Playskills 2
Real Children at Play 5
The Mythical Child 7
Teachers of Play 8
Teaching Techniques 9

Chapter 2: Imitative Play 15
Uses of Imitative Play Drills 15
Imitative Play Drill Techniques 15
Use of Imitative Play Targets 18
Imitative Play Targets 19
Independent Play 30

Chapter 3: Manipulatives and Building 35
Wooden Blocks 35
Duplos 36
Legos 39
Other Building Materials 41

Chapter 4: Toy Play 43
Closed-End Toys 43
Puzzles 45
Construction Toys 46
Open-End Toys and Vehicles 47

Chapter 5: In Vivo Pretend Play 51
Single-Action Pretend 51
Daily Routines and Familiar Activities 54
Places to Go 54
Dress Up and Character Pretend 55
Pretend Play Centers and Social Pretend Play .63

Chapter 6: In Vitro Pretend Play 73
Types of Figurines 74
Playsets 74
Individual Characters 76

Progression of Figurine Play 77
    Figurine Scenes 77
    Figurine Action Pretend with Narration .77
    Talking for Figurines 78
    Social Figurine Play 78

Chapter 7: Games 81
Social Games and Classic Children's Games 81
Music and Song Games 86
Turn-Taking Games 88
Board Games 88
Games Tutor Notes 90

Chapter 8: Music 97
Materials 97
Teaching Procedures 98
Song Lists 99

Chapter 9: Sensory and Physical Play 103
Playdough and Clay 103
Putty and Slime 108
Gross Motor Play Activities 109
Ball Play 111

Chapter 10: Water and Sand Play 113
Water Play 113
Exploratory Water Play 114
Water Painting and Art Activities 115
Water Pretend Activities 116
Social Water Games 116
Water Parks 117
Sand Play 118
Sensory Activities and Exploratory Play 120
Sand Pretend Activities 121
Sand Building 121
Sand Art 122
Sensory Box 122

Chapter 11: Arts and Crafts 123
The Craft Box 123
General Suggestions for Arts and Crafts Projects 124
Craft Ideas 125
Craft Recipes 126
Craft Resources 127

Chapter 12: Playdates 129
Early Peer Interactions 129
Playdates Versus Playgroups 130
Playdate Goals 131
Playdate Prerequisites 132
Playdate Peers 133
The Playdate Pool 134
Types of Peers 135
Peer Preparation 136
Playdate Structure 138
Early Playdates 138
Evolving Playdates 139
The Theme Structure 140
The Preschool Structure 141
Unstructured Playdates 141

Chapter 13: Playgroups 143
Playgroup Goals and Alternatives 143
Playgroup Peers 145
Playgroup Structure 146
Playdate/Playgroup Themes 147
Free Social Play 148

Chapter 14: Playgroup and Playdate Themes 151
Play Theme-Based Activities 151
Suggested Activities and Materials for Selected Themes 154

Chapter 15: School-Aged Children 159
Television and Videos 160
Video Games 165
Cooking 165
Other Activities for School-Aged Children 167

Bibliography 169

Companies and Products 171

Preface

I was introduced to the world of autism in January 1998. After two years of frustration and heartache trying to deal with my child's lack of language and his uncontrollable behavior, it finally dawned on me that he had some form of developmental delay. Several months earlier, after a single consultation, his developmental pediatrician had given him the diagnosis of:

1. Severe expressive and receptive language delay
2. Atypical behavior patterns
3. Atypical social interactions

He recommended a special preschool language class twice a week and speech therapy once a week.

My child started this minimal therapy, and I started to read and research. As I read the millions of pages in print and on the Internet about developmental delay, those three statements began to scream one thing at me: Autistic Spectrum Disorder (ASD).

In February 1998, I asked my developmental pediatrician about the diagnosis and he said that, yes, my child was on the spectrum. However, no further recommendations for treatment were forthcoming.

Adrenaline-charged panic set in, and my frenzied search for information accelerated. By absolute web-surfing chance, I found out about ABA (Applied Behavioral Analysis) therapy; and by even more website digging, I found a phone number of a woman who gave me the phone number to another woman who was starting to consult for ABA therapy locally.

I contacted her, and after a four-month wait, we were off on an intense forty-hour-a-week home program that lasted for two years. For two years, tutors and consultants roamed my house seven days a week; for two years; I spent every night and weekend after work organizing the program book, troubleshooting problems, writing comments, searching for supplies, searching for tutors, training tutors, paying tutors, reading books, reading thousands of e-mail messages on my internet mailing lists, running team meetings and workshops, organizing materials, watching videos of my child in therapy in his room, trying to do therapy myself, and e-mailing updates to the consultant. For two years I was in a state of agony and worry.

My child learned a lot during those two years, and so did I. I learned how truly painful mistakes can be. I learned to pick my battles. I learned the difference between the appearance of doing something and actually doing it. I learned to love my child intensely for who he is and not what I think he should be. I learned to laugh at my child and be charmed by him. I learned to ignore a disapproving public.

Part of my child's therapy involved teaching playskills. We found that teaching my child play was very difficult because we were adults and had forgotten how to play. I picked up a toy or figurine and was absolutely stumped about how to proceed with it or how to teach my child to play with it. I don't know why we lose that ability. Perhaps as adults we think of the steps involved as so simple as not to be worth thinking about, but it was an odd feeling holding a lump of clay in my hand and being absolutely stalled in proceeding to teach my child how to play with it.

We tried to teach many types of play with my child. Some attempts were more successful than others. I learned much about what was appropriate and what was not appropriate for preschool children to do. I learned that play is ultimately personal. Not all children play in the same way or with the same things, just as no adults have exactly the same leisure activities and hobbies. I learned there is no child who plays perfectly. I learned to let go of the image of children playing quietly together in some idealized Victorian nursery setting (playgroups experiences disabused me of that notion in a hurry).

This book comes from those lessons. It is aimed at parents who are teaching playskills to their preschool or early school-age child. It is a practical manual that you can refer to when you are teaching play to your child. You can put it next to you while you are playing with your child and get ideas to jump-start your imagination. The book will, I hope, help put the play arena into perspective. It offers you flexibility in what to teach, based on what your child enjoys and what is developmentally appropriate.

Although I am a medical doctor, I am by no means an expert in developmental delay. I included some academic thoughts about play in my introduction to help guide you in what experts do consider appropriate development of play according to their research. These classifications of play should not be considered as definitive; rather they should guide you when you assess your child and decide what types of play you are going to teach.

In addition, I have included ideas and insights that I have accumulated from talking with parents, from surfing the net, from attending workshops, and from talking with tutors and therapists. Every attempt has been made to credit sources, but the ideas have come from so many informal interactions that crediting them all has been impossible. In many cases, parents who shared ideas with me wish to remain anonymous. The major source by far is my own interaction with and observations of my son as I have attempted to teach him how to play.

Highlighted within boxes scattered throughout the text are excerpts from parents who have given permission for me to include their first-person accounts of working with their own children. The writers of these passages, which are in Italics, have not been identified. In addition, I have included some examples of notes taken by tutors of my own child. They also appear in boxes. I hope that the parents' observations can help you understand that many others share your frustrations and that your child behaves in many of the same ways as other ASD children. I included the tutors' notes to help you understand that keeping such records can help you chart progress as well as identifying areas that need more attention.

Ultimately, I hope this manual will be useful to you on a day-to-day basis, a guide you can carry with you into the therapy room or to the playground.

Chapter 1
Teaching Playskills

- *Definitions of Play*
- *The Development of Playskills*
- *Real Children at Play*
- *The Mythical Child*
- *Teachers of Play*
- *Teaching Techniques*

When adults watch children at play, they are usually delighted to be drawn back into their own memories of childhood, reliving happy moments of childhood play. When the parents of children with Autistic Spectrum Disorder (ASD) watch other children play, they frequently become overwhelmed with grief. This sadness can be so extreme as to make the simple act of sitting at a playground unbearable. Watching other children play deepens the sense of loss we feel for our children—a loss of friends, of curiosity, of imagination, and of fun—a loss of childhood itself. When we teach playskills to our ASD children, we are trying to restore that gift of childhood, while providing some foundational skills for generalized learning throughout life.

As a part of childhood, play serves many functions. Children may practice language and social skills in a relatively safe environment where mistakes are tolerated and repetition of the practice develops confidence and competence. Children may begin learning the rudiments of abstract thought, flexibility, and creativity, while practicing and learning the concept of "rules." The need for negotiation and compromise in play helps develop empathy and supports the development of friendships. Finally, play for play itself may provide some stress relief for our children, whose childhoods are filled with days of difficult demands.

Autistic Spectrum Disorder children with no ability to play or those who can play in only stereotypical and obsessive ways are obviously deprived of all the learning and enjoyment that occur during normal play. In addition, because of their abnormal behavior, they are frequently excluded from peer play or, worse, subjected to abuse and teasing. If a child becomes isolated in this way during early childhood, he or she is thrown into a vicious cycle of rejection and increasing social incompetence, compounding his or her isolation during life.

Teaching playskills in a systematic and structured way gives the child the tools to play independently and ultimately interact with peers. This systematic teaching helps the child avoid social rejection and frustration by giving the child the skills that allow him or her to be perceived by other children as a competent player. These skills should set the stage for a lifetime of play both in social settings and in solitary leisure activities.

DEFINITIONS OF PLAY

Although most adults think they know what constitutes play, few can really define it. Although the definition of *play* varies greatly from discipline to discipline, several descriptive and distinctive features of play can be identified. Childhood play, as described by Pamela Wolfberg and Adriana L. Schuler (1992), happens voluntarily, often spontaneously, offering the child internal reinforcements and rewards. Play is active, valued by the players, novel, and non-rigid. Wolfberg and Schuler also describe play as having ever-expanding themes, having distinct indications that the players know the difference between reality and pretend, and as having an organization imposed by the players. These features of play in normal children can help one compare it with the play of children with Autistic Spectrum Disorder (ASD).

In contrast, the play of ASD children tends to be ritualistic, stereotypical, and repetitive. It is often without social engagement and can be self-stimulatory in nature. This play has an element of rigidity characterized by a resistance to change in play routines coupled with a tendency towards *echo-play-lia* (a pun on *echolalia* coined by Wolfberg to describe a literal imitation of a play sequence) rather than spontaneous and imaginative play.

The autistic kids basically like the same toys as typical kids but they are more repetitive in their play, they are more obsessive, and they are less eager to have anyone else involved. Those differences can be worked on, but also it must be remembered that typical kids can be repetitive (typical kids might line up cars too, but they wouldn't do it all day). They can also seem obsessive; there are some real Pokemon-iacs out there who know everything about Pokemon and two of them are my typical kids. However, most typical kids are happy to have a playmate even if the children will be fighting minutes after starting to play together. One of the first play differences I noticed with Robbie, my typical fifth child, who is younger than Putter (ASD), was that Robbie, like Putter, adored balls, but Putter would kick or throw the ball and run after it himself. Robbie would pick up the ball and look for a person.

Childhood play consists of a wide variety of activities that include physical, social, and cognitive components. A specific activity may have several overlapping components, but to design appropriate teaching programs, it is nevertheless helpful to think about what components an activity contains. Physical play elements appear in such activities as building with blocks and other manipulatives, working puzzles, and participating in fine motor games, exercise, gross motor activities, physical social games, sports, and the physical leisure activities of later childhood and adulthood. Cognitive and creative play elements are seen in toy play, pretend and imaginative play, games, mental puzzles, art projects, and music. Social play elements are seen in social games and pretend and in group and cooperative projects as well as in conversation.

THE DEVELOPMENT OF PLAYSKILLS

The development of play in children has been classified in several ways. Different researchers have emphasized different parts of play. To give an idea of the variety of play and some sense of how it develops, I include here two of the many schemes described by researchers (see especially Garvey, 1977; Piaget, 1962; Rubin, Fein & Vandenberg, 1983; Vygotsky, 1978, Westby, 1991, and Wolfberg *et al*, 1992). To have a thorough understanding of play development, you should be familiar with a variety of classifications. These classifications can then serve as general guides to the level of the child's development and need for intervention.

PLAY DEVELOPMENT

This scheme shows play developing in the following broad areas through overlapping and parallel stages. That is, these playskills don't occur one after the other but develop concurrently in different areas. This classification concentrates on the development of social play with adults and peers. The schema is adapted from Pamela Wolfberg and Adriana L. Schuler's classification in their resource manual *Integrated Play Groups* (1992).

Interactive Play with Adults. This kind of play begins with the child's initial passive observation of an adult playing both roles of a social interaction. By playing both roles, the adult simulates a real social interaction. The most common form of early social play with adults is the game of Peek-a-Boo, according to Wolfberg and Schuler. In this game, the child must be watching the adult in an interested way. The adult covers his or her face and then uncovers it, saying "Peek-a-Boo—I see you!" with very animated expressions and a vocal tone that prompts the child to smile or laugh. This early form of turn-taking with the parent's eliciting a response is repeated over and over until the child becomes more sophisticated and, in anticipation of the surprise, starts smiling and laughing when the adult first covers his or her face. The child begins to understand the rhythm of the game and increasingly participates—starting to cover his or her own face and taking turns with the surprise. This turn-taking then evolves into new game sequences invented by the child for play with adults. The child might repeat a simple reciprocal play sequence many times, as the adult learns his or her role. For example, the child might repeatedly hide as the parent (who can see the child behind the chair) says, "Where's Tim? — Oh NO — where's Tim?" and the child pops out and says, "Here I am!"

Interactive Play with Peers. In contrast to early social play with adults, early play with peers begins with parallel play and then evolves to reciprocal and cooperative play. Parallel play begins with a child playing solitarily in the proximity of another child. This play progresses from an awareness of other children playing nearby—with no interaction—to the imitation of one another, and finally to progressively longer and more sophisticated interactions among the children. At first, children playing in parallel may just tolerate each another's presence. Eventually, they may watch each other briefly, and progress to exchanging toys, playing with a toy at the same time, and occasionally imitating each other's toy play. Their interactions become progressively longer and more social as they develop.

Play with Objects. Playing with objects begins with the child's learning about an object by putting it into his or her mouth and banging the object against something; and then this kind of play progresses to a more conventional use of toys. Typical children in the first year of life explore toys in a repetitious or random fashion. The child first handles all objects in the same way, exploring them by looking at them, mouthing them, listening to them, moving, shaking, or banging them, or feeling them with different parts of the body.

The second stage of this kind of play occurs when the child starts working on spatial relationships by stacking objects or nesting them or transferring them in and out of containers. The child may start taking apart combinations of objects by dismantling snap together toys or interlocking beads. As the child develops, he or she uses toys in more conventional ways. For example, instead of chewing on a toy car or shaking it, a child might start to roll it back and forth on the floor. As the child becomes even more sophisticated with toys, he or she is able to sequence actions with toys spatially and temporally and manipulate them appropriately. The child can now put pieces into simple puzzles or string beads, for example, or manipulate a toy that requires a sequence of actions for it to work.

Pretend Play. Early pretend play usually involves reenactments of familiar routines such as eating with play food or drinking from an empty cup, cooking in a play kitchen, playing house, or playing with a baby doll by rocking it or putting it in bed. Later the child might engage in dress-up and pretend to be a dog, a doctor, or a popular fantasy superhero. Objects used in play (symbols) can evolve from being very concrete and similar to the real item to being much more symbolic. For example the child may progress from using a plastic toy play telephone to using a simple wooden block to represent a phone and finally to pretending to talk on the phone without any props at all. As the child's understanding increases, he or she is able to have almost any object represent another object. For example, the child might put a bowl on his or her head and use it as a hat or use a broom to represent a horse. The child might even be able to create imaginary objects and describe them. I call these types of activities *in vivo* pretend play because the child is using his or her body to pretend. The child's is "in the play," pretending to be someone or something he or she is not or is engaging in an activity with pretend objects.

Highly developed symbolic pretend play involves figurines (dolls, puppets, or other representations of animate objects). At the highest level of figurine play, the child moves and talks for the figure as if the figure could initiate its own actions and talk for itself. In this sort of pretend, the figurine has its own personality, and the child is not "in the play." I call this type of pretend activity *in vitro* because the child is not using his or her own body to pretend; he or she is pretending through a representation of an animate object. Early *in vitro* pretend starts with the child's holding a figurine and perhaps identifying it. Then, the child may start moving a figurine and manipulating it through a series of actions. Later, he or she might talk for the figure, and the child might even have two or more figurines talking to one another. Finally, he or she might be able to engage in reciprocal social figurine play with another child.

Pretend Play with Peers. This type of play is the most common kind of pretend play in preschool and kindergarten. This is the world of "make believe" where children act out plays and create pretend worlds based on their own lives, popular fictional characters, and totally invented characters. This type of pretend play progresses from solitary dress-up activities. At this stage, children prefer to play this way with peers rather than alone by assigning roles and acting out situations. The children may act out shopping at a store, eating at a restaurant, or camping in the woods. Language is frequently sophisticated and complex. In this type of play children learn many social skills.

Play in Later Childhood. In later childhood, games with rules seem to dominate play through formal games, sports, board games, card games, and video games (see Piaget, 1962, as well as Bergen and Oden, 1988). Some pretend play may still go on, but it tends to fade as children begin spending lots of time together, talking and conversing, exploring, participating in such physical activities as roller skating and biking, and enjoying formal after-school activities.

The ABLLS Classification

Another guide to the development of play in children is The Assessment of Basic Language and Learning Skills (ABLLS). This assessment tool analyzes skills of children with autism and other developmental disabilities, and it presents a guide for helping these children develop many kinds of academic, motor, and social skills, including play (see Partington and Sundberg 52-53). It also provides an outline for charting the child's progress. In the progression of playskills it describes the child:

➢ Investigates toys and handles them appropriately;
➢ Differentiates themes suggested by toys and performs several theme-related activities with them;
➢ Plays independently and talks while playing;
➢ Plays with other children, exchanging toys as the children request and continuing to play in close proximity to other children;
➢ Talks to other children while playing with them;
➢ Pretends to be another person and performs activities appropriate for that role;
➢ Plays both indoor and outdoor games, including board games and sports games, appropriately.

Like Pamela Wolfberg's developmental scheme of play, the ABLLS classification describes both solitary object play as well as social interaction with other children and adults.

Use the above classifications to assess where your child is developmentally and to help plan his or her play programs. Keep in mind that one characteristic of ASD is the splintering of skills. When you assess the child, you might find him or her being very advanced in one area of play while not able to participate in another area at all. This skill-splintering suggests that it is important to allow the child to play in a range of developmental levels. The child might chronologically age out of an activity before he or she is developmentally finished with it. Be flexible and allow an older child to continue to play dress-up, for example, while you are teaching him or her older-child playskills like board games.

REAL CHILDREN AT PLAY

Although the above classifications help determine where a child is developmentally in the physical, cognitive, functional, and social dimensions of play, your most important source of information for teaching the child is other children. It is important that you observe how the child's peers play because frequently they don't play by the book. To know what to teach, you need to know what the other children are playing. In particular I think it is imperative for women running home programs for boys to observe other typical boys at play and make sure that they are not imposing inappropriate activities of their girlhood play on their male children.

The type of play I see at school in a preschool setting is different than the type of play I see at home. The type of play I see on the playground is also different than the type of play I see in a structured playgroup setting. Consultants and parents who are running their own programs can run into a danger of being out of touch with the population of typical children. This is because they fill their day working with the ASD child. They might go in and observe the play of the ASD child in a naturalized setting but I get the impression that quite a few people only do it in a school setting. Our preschool had strict rules about violent play (yes, being a construction worker and pretending to knock down a Lincoln log house was deemed violent and our shadow was promptly disciplined for teaching the kids to do it!) This rule about violent play, however, did not carry over to play group. The kids went home and did it. I think that consultants and those without other kids should routinely go to McDonald's, the kids' sections at bookstores, and public parks, and observe what the typical kids are doing.

Observe Your Other Children

Having older (or younger) children usually helps a parent to observe how typical children play. Unfortunately, siblings do not always play typically themselves, and observing their play can be misleading. For example, my older typical child was heavily into figurine pretend play. He could play by himself or with another child for hours using various figurines and scenes that constantly varied and flowed seamlessly into long complicated situations. He talked for his figurines constantly and had them act out various scenarios. He frequently had me videotape his plays. I soon found out, however, that this extremely sophisticated and highly developed figurine pretend play was not typical for my older son's male peers. Only one child that he knew could play with him in this fashion. None of the boys that my older child played with were interested in or capable of this sort of play. Usually, however, siblings provide an excellent reference for the type and variety of play activities that the child's peers are playing.

My child's typical sibling is 5.5 and is attending kindergarten. He is completely into Digimon (his interest used to be Pokemon). This is definitely his favorite activity — playing with the characters, looking at Digimon books, etc. He is into pretend play and has a dress-up box full of various clothing options. In addition to pretending he is someone (again, a Digimon or super hero), he likes to pretend that he is going somewhere like camping or on vacation. He also loves to play games (card games, Connect Four, Hands Down, Junior Yahtzee), put together puzzles, and color. During recess at school he seems just to run a lot with the other boys (and some girls), playing chasing games or pretending they are Digimon characters or superhero characters.

Observe Other Children

Although it is very important to observe other children at play, also remember that many children these days are so hurried that they are moved from formal activity to formal activity at a very young age (i.e., Suzuki at age three, soccer at age four). Many children have highly structured days and might not have the opportunity just to relax and pretend. Whether you think this scheduling is good or bad is not the point. The point is that you need to know what the other children are doing and what is considered appropriate. When you start participating in playdates, you might be surprised at how little exposure to and practice with free pretend play your child's peers have.

What I have learned from watching my neighbor's typical sons (5 and almost 3) is that boys are repetitive. They play the same thing over and over again. The dinosaurs chase and eat each other. They fight. They chase each other around the house screaming. They like to play swords. They hit when they don't get their way. They take other people's toys. They are selfish. I guess what I am trying to say is don't overestimate typical children. I have yet to meet a 3-4 year-old who plays nicely. They do still mostly parallel play while interacting a little. But no elaborate play schemes.

Observe Preschool Classrooms

Visit preschools to see what your child will be playing with in the classroom. I recall taking my Barbie doll to kindergarten, but I have not seen that sort of flexibility in the preschools my children attended. Usually, the teacher sets up the room, and the children move from center to center during free time, choosing their activities from those furnished by the school. Typical activities that the children participated in during free time (in my sons' preschool and kindergarten) included:

Blocks and building—both as solitary and cooperative activities

Pretend Play Centers—usually a kitchen where the children can pretend to cook, eat, and serve food

Dress-up and role-play—doctor, vet, construction worker
Arts and crafts—frequently with a holiday or a seasonal theme
Toy play—Cars, trucks, pretend items, animal figurines

If your child goes to preschool, have your tutors or shadows take notes on the play of the children, noting what they played with, how long, what sort of language they used, and how the play evolved. Also have them note the general attention spans of your child's peers and the responsiveness of the children to one another.

After we had taught what we thought was a great set of play skills, we realized that kids do not play at all like we taught. Once we started to look a bit more we realized that a lot of things we were pushing so much (eye contact, full sentences, etc.) were not something that typical kids did. So we made a new rule for the kids I work with. Before we start teaching anything, we look at kids their ages to gauge how we need to teach. For example, we had taught, "give me that, please" when someone took something from you. When I went to observe at preschool, I saw that kids were more likely to say, "Hey, give that back" or "That was mine." So we went back and re-taught some things to make our kid sound and look much more typical.

THE MYTHICAL CHILD

Direct observation of typical kids in a variety of situations will help you avoid creating in your mind the image of a child who plays perfectly, who is socially aware, who is kind and caring. This child does not exist. Do not expect your child to be transformed into this mythical being. Children, even typical ones, need to be taught to play nicely, to share, to cooperate, and to empathize. When you begin peer play with your child, don¹t be caught off-guard by rude, demanding, self-absorbed normal children. They will be learning mature behavior along with your child.

When I think of my child, I think of a child that is just "more." Everything is "more." He is more intense. More happy. More sad. More. He is more fidgety. He is more angry. He is more intelligent. He is more sensitive. He is more. He has more language deficits. He has more vocabulary words than the average child does. His play is often more creative. His play is often more rigid. He is more impulsive. He is more spontaneous. He is more concerned with the details. He is more careless. He is just plain old more.

My playgroup experiences made me realize that I had truly created a mythical child in my mind. The mythical child sits nicely for circle time—legs crossed, hands folded in lap, eyes on teacher. The mythical child builds forts and has play scenarios that last hours. The mythical child listens the first time. The mythical child reads his peers and acts on this reading instantly. The mythical child does not say "no." The mythical child is quiet. The mythical child does not fidget. The mythical child never does anything weird.

The mythical child blends. He can camouflage himself. The mythical child does not stare out the window or play with the string hanging on his shirt. He does not suck his hands or pick his nose. The mythical child never puts anything in his mouth. The mythical child does not leave the bathroom door open when he pees. He would never think to pee on a tree. The mythical child picks his toys up without nagging. Heck, the mythical child picks his toys up without being told. The mythical child loves sports and will play catch with dad every evening. He plays little league in the spring and soccer at the "Y" in the fall. He plays basketball in the winter. He sings "Jesus loves all the little children" at Bible school in the summer.

The mythical child is less. Less intense. Less happy. Less angry. The mythical child never visits a mental la-la land. The mythical child is less work. The mythical child is in black and white, complete with his own theme song.

TEACHERS OF PLAY

Children generally learn early playskills from adults. Social play with adults, using games such as Peek-a-Boo and Pat-a-Cake, form the earliest play experiences for babies. Adult teachers of play in the developmentally delayed child's life include parents and tutors who are trained to break down tasks properly and reinforce the child. These adults are trained to deal with the child and motivate him or her so that the child does not engage in tantrums and task avoidance. However, relying exclusively on parents and tutors to teach play can become problematic because frequently these adults have forgotten how to play and can impose very odd play onto developmentally delayed children, projecting idealized, genteel, politically correct situations and themes onto a toddler who has no social motivation. This inappropriate play can result in some embarrassingly bizarre consequences when the child is eventually put into play situations with active, imperfect, ill mannered, semi-socially developed (but totally normal) peers.

It is critical for adults who teach play to know the development of normal play in children and also to be aware of *what exactly it is that they are teaching.* I have seen many situations in which the "props of play" are used to teach non-play characteristics like social behavior, self-control, and good manners. This process is all well and fine if these lessons are what you consciously are trying to teach, but you should not label the act of role-playing a social situation with an adult an act of play.

Another problem with adults teaching play is the physical limitations that some people develop as they age. If you are not willing to get muddy or wet and you get winded playing a game of tag, you need to find someone who can play physically with your child. Sitting for thirty minutes and doing circle time activities might be all you can handle, but it is *not* play.

Other people who teach play to the child should include young adults who have no physical limitations. Once your child has developed some playskills, find some young adults or teenagers whose only task is to play with the child. These young people are removed somewhat from the formal therapy situation and frequently are seen as simply fun and reinforcing to the child. A play tutor who can take your child swimming or to the park or who will push him or her on a bike can be very helpful.

Children would seem like natural teachers of play to other children, but they usually don't have the size, skills, or maturity to teach early playskills. However, peers will become critical components in your child's later play program and need to be introduced as soon as possible. You will probably start out with somewhat older children who have been prepared to deal with your child. These first interactions will be more therapy-like and stilted. As soon as you are able, you will need to introduce into play untrained peers of different ages, school peers, siblings, siblings' friends, unknown children at public places, and groups of children.

TEACHING TECHNIQUES

First, I have to say that language instruction has a clear priority over play instruction. Language will give your child many tools with which to learn everything else, including play. Make sure that the child's intervention program has language instruction as its key intervention. Your child has to have at least the ability to communicate desires in some form using speech, Picture Exchange Communication System (PECS), or sign language, so that his or her frustration won't come out in unwanted behaviors. Remember that the earliest form of social motivation for children is to satisfy their own needs and wants, and your child needs to be able to do just that.

Language skills are essential to playskills in the slightly older child (age 4-6) and if this child has pronoun confusion or syntax problems, peers are not as keen on patiently waiting until the child spits it out. How do you create major pretend play scenarios with a child whose speech is a jumbled mess? Playskills and language skills are not entirely separate entities. While we teach them separately, they must be combined as a whole in the real world outside the therapy room.

Once you have established intensive language intervention, then assess the child's current level of play, using the various classifications above and your own observations of the child's siblings and peers. Assess the child's functional use of objects, level of social motivation, physical capabilities, social capacity, interests, and daily schedule.

Play is very personal, offering a wide variety of activities for children. I think it is important to stick initially with the basics—the classic types of toys and activities that children have played with for many years. In addition, give your child depth in a classic game such as Red Light, Green Light, so that he or she is a good player, rather than spreading the child's learning over dozens of games so that he or she cannot play a single one well.

Learn to "mine" an interest. You can use a single theme to teach a variety of playskills. If the child shows an interest in a theme, then find ways to expand on the theme, teaching many different playskills using the same theme. Finding a child's interest and expanding on it will improve motivation and ease reinforcement. This teaching is not "child-led" but rather child-themed. The child decides the material and you decide what is taught.

For example, if the child becomes interested in *Star Wars* by watching the movie, you have a variety of teaching possibilities and activities available. These include:

Star Wars Legos—manipulative imitation, building, fine motor, pretend, sequencing, multiple component discrimination
Star Wars costumes—pretend play, dress-up, pretend play center play

Star Wars figurines and vehicles—figurine pretend, miniature play, imagination
Star Wars puzzles, games, art projects, and books
Star Wars at the movie theater—community behavior, conversation, anticipation
Star Wars videos— language development, music listening skills, community behavior, renting, buying

Teaching Techniques

I am not a formally accredited expert, and I do not have any data or evidence that the programs and techniques discussed in this book are the best available or that they will work for your child. I and the other parents I have talked with, however, have experienced the results of intense intervention with our own children. My desire is to present specific and practical ideas that will help you in improving your child's success with this major part of life. Because of the limited time frame for early intervention, nothing frustrates parents of ASD children more than to have to create one's own therapy laboriously and reinvent the wheel while precious time slips away. I also have some perspective that comes from hard experience, and I hope that you can use it avoid some of the mistakes that I have made. The ideas in this book have been used in various programs. Some worked better than others. Not all will be appropriate for your child.

This book is based on the experience of teaching using Applied Behavioral Analysis (ABA) techniques. These techniques can be adapted to other types of teaching programs, but much of the language as well as the methods of presentation and teaching is specific to ABA programs. If you are currently involved in such a program, it is best to work with your own consultant to find for your child the most appropriate mode of presentation of the targets that are discussed. The drills and techniques in this book should be individualized for your child's particular strengths and interests.

In a systematic program for teaching playskills, complex play behaviors that come naturally to most children are analyzed so that their components can be taught step by step in an organized way. To teach these complex behaviors, the teacher must break down each behavior into component steps as small and incremental as are needed to teach the child. If the child is having difficulty learning, then the teacher must reassess the target behavior and analyze the point where the child is having difficulty and modify the procedure, the incremental step, or the reinforcement to enhance learning. Repetition is also heavily emphasized. Our children frequently need to repeat appropriate behaviors many times before the behaviors become part of their repertoire. This method is not so much different from the ways in which a person learns other behaviors in life. After all, a person can't learn to play basketball by reading the rulebook! Breaking down the game of basketball into its separate physical skills and practicing them in isolation prior to integrating them into game play is a normal part of becoming a competent player. However, when one breaks down a part of life that is supposed to be innate and natural, like dividing play into teachable steps, the incremental components, viewed individually, will seem forced and unnatural. To parents of children already in intense ABA programs, this point does not need to be belabored. But for those unfamiliar with ABA or those not running a similar home program, it may seem paradoxical to use highly structured and directed techniques to teach what we hope is ultimately natural and unstructured play, both alone and with peers.

Teaching techniques may vary from program to program, but we used a base of *imitative teaching* for all types of play, expanding simple imitation into more sophisticated reciprocal play and finally working on developing a true give and take between the tutor and child. All sorts of different types of play can be taught initially with an imitative base (See Figure 1).

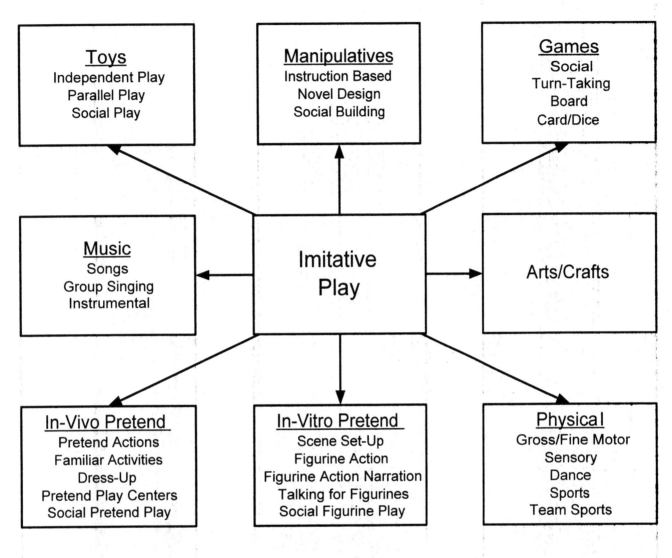

Figure 1

We started imitative teaching with discrete trial techniques (DTT) at the therapy table to show our child specific things to do with various materials and toys. But once he had a few items under his belt, we moved to the floor and then outside the therapy room to start changing the focus of the instruction from strict imitative drills to real play. It is a delicate (and sometimes long and difficult) transition from the adult-led structure of ABA teaching to the child-led activities of normal play and finally to the peer-led and interactive play that we would all like our children to be able to participate in.

The eventual goal of structured instruction is self-reinforcing, creative, enjoyable, unstructured play performed by our children alone and with their friends. The only way to achieve this goal is to work relentlessly to reduce the initial structure as much as possible and increase the child's internal motivation so that he or she wants to play "because I have fun" and not "because I get an M&M." Intense and individualized reinforcement for appropriate behaviors will increase the child's motivation and create a self-perpetuating desire to play and interact.

Reinforcement is the key to teaching success. Play is self-reinforcing to normal children. However, in our ASD kids, this self-reinforcement for normal play is usually absent. At first, we have to provide the motivation to play and interact in the form of external reinforcement. Appropriate reinforcement is critical to teaching ASD children. It has been said that boredom is not in the task; it is in the reinforcer or motivation. We do not find a task boring if the reinforcement is high enough. We humans will engage in the most mundane and repetitive of tasks if there is an appropriate reinforcer for it—for example, working a slot machine. Teaching a play activity is more complicated because we want our children to be reinforced by the activity itself. We are trying to make play and social interaction become self-reinforcing for the child.

To understand how to reinforce play (and other types of social behavior), one must realize that there is a progressive development of what motivates children to engage in social activities. This social motivation, which develops slowly in normal children, seems to stall completely in our children. The development of social motivation begins with the child being motivated only by his or her own needs and desires. At some point, however, the typical child develops the social motivation to please his parents. The desire to please other people is an even more advanced stage of social motivation. Ultimately, the child is motivated by a sense of self-pride in his or her behavior.

It's a long, long journey from egocentric motivation to a motivation to have pride in oneself. This process may take several years. In teaching playskills, it is important to understand this sequence so that you aren't trying to get your child to do something for which he or she has not developed the internal social motivation to do (i.e., "Make Mommy happy" or "Play nicely with your friend or he will think you don't like him"). It is important to work on appropriate reinforcement no matter what your child's level of social motivation.

Without appropriately motivating the child, you will experience all the trauma of noncompliance: tantrums, inattention, and running away. You will need to provide the appropriate level of external reinforcement until the child's internal social motivation starts to take over.

While it is possible to learn many things through external nonsocial motivation, it is difficult, if not impossible, for the child to develop spontaneous joint attention (two or more people attending to something together), and advanced observational learning without the appropriate level of social motivation. As you work towards this level, you will need to tailor your reinforcement to the motivation at work in your child at that time. It might be very artificial for a long time ("Play nicely and you get an ice cream cone")—but the hope is that eventually, with positively reinforced social interactions with peers, the child will be reinforced by the social interaction itself.

When the child becomes reinforced by social interaction, then social motivation becomes self-perpetuating. Improved social motivation will lead to more social interactions. Increased social interactions will lead to higher social motivation. The result is improved play skills from increasing peer interactions and reciprocal activities.

In the beginning of play programs, even the child's own stereotypical and repetitive play can be used for motivational purposes. You can start with an obsession (running sand through your fingers) and use that as your motivator as you vary and expand sand play. You are not allowing the child to continue to play obsessively; you are using the obsession to get the child started with a material or activity and intervening to direct the child to more appropriate play, preserving some of the reinforcing stimulus (the feel of sand). Even painting mirrors with spit can be a start if you are able to transfer the tactile obsession to finger-painting. String and rope obsessions can provide the start for pretend play (snakes and fishing) and physical activities (jump rope and limbo).

Finally, even with all your preparation and teaching, you will ultimately have to allow your child to experience play and make mistakes. Children are experiential learners. There are some things in life that you can't explain to your children. They have to experience it. This reality means that your child will most likely experience some episodes of social rejection and will display inappropriate behavior in public places. You must steel yourself for the inevitable stares and muttering of an uninformed populace and remind yourself that you are teaching the child, not an anonymous crowd.

Chapter 2
Imitative Play

- *Uses of Imitative Play Drills*
- *Imitative Play Drill Techniques*
- *Use of Imitative Play Targets*
- *Imitative Play Targets*
- *Independent Play*

USE OF IMITATIVE PLAY DRILLS

Imitative play drills can create a core set of skills in your child's playskills program. Imitative play drills really strengthen the imitation skills that can lead to observational learning. They are not an end unto themselves but rather serve as a launch point to other skills. The many uses of imitative play drills include:

➤ To improve imitative skills
➤ To demonstrate the various methods of play
➤ To allow your child to experience different forms of play
➤ To discover your child's interests
➤ To stimulate brainstorming
➤ To form a base for expansion into other areas of play
➤ To begin the evolution from imitation to observational learning from a peer

I have never directly taught Justin (ASD, almost 4) how to play. The only things I have taught him are things you would have to teach any child. I showed him how to bat, how to shoot a basket, how to kick a ball, how to hit a golf ball and a hockey puck. We taught him how to ride a tricycle/bicycle and how to rollerblade. Mostly he learned all these skills by imitation. We showed him, he watched, he did what we showed him.

IMITATIVE PLAY DRILL TECHNIQUES

Imitative drills are demonstrative drills. Imitative play drills involve nonverbal and verbal imitation with toys, activities, and verbalizations. These drills can be started at the very beginning of a program: nonverbal imitation is one of the earliest drills in ABA programs. The tutor says, "Do this" or something similar and then demonstrates the action and/or verbalization. The child is prompted to *imitate* his or her actions and verbalizations. We started these drills in discrete trial training (DTT) format at the table and then moved to the floor. The tutor tried to avoid "instructing" verbally, saying simply "Do this" (imitation) rather than giving a specific instruction (receptive language). When the child knows a few items under each activity, start chaining them together as a sequence of actions.

Imitative play can serve as a testing ground to reveal your child's interests. Rather than forcing your child to play with every toy made or to participate in every activity known to childhood, you present him or her with a variety of actions and toys and try them out. If, at some point in training, the child becomes interested in a toy or activity and does a spontaneous action with it, then you can celebrate and allow him or her to take the lead briefly. Imitate the child and work towards a real give-and-take situation between tutor and child, one in which they alternate between leading and following.

In addition, this method of imitative teaching ("Do this") makes the child actually do the action rather than passively observe the action. This experiential learning is easier for a child than watching or hearing the tutor explain things to him or her. It also does not require that the child be able to follow complex oral instructions.

Teaching a child imitation skills as they relate to toys can have an effect on inappropriate play as well. The child can now go to a toy that has been taught and pick it up and do something appropriate with it (instead of rubbing it on his or her face or shaking it).

You can also view these drills as a brainstorming technique for creating play targets. In the beginning, the parent will be creating the targets, but this process should evolve to the point where the tutor is ad-libbing new targets during therapy. One hopes the child will start to ad-lib targets as well (these actions are written down and reinforced the next time that activity is done). Next the tutor and child will start to give and take—each suggesting things to do. When a peer is introduced, the same interaction can take place, with the peer leading, then the child, back and forth.

Another important goal of these imitative play drills is to give the child the ability to go up to a group of kids doing something (typical preschool center-time), watch them, imitate what they are doing, and suggest new actions. Being familiar with the toy or activity also allows him or her to join in the play even if the child is not yet able to hold a sustained conversation about it.

> *My child is somewhat verbal and he is just beginning to imitate other children at the playground. He watches a child dig sand like a dog (digging between their legs) and he imitates that. When a child runs out of the wading pool or pretends to be an alligator, he will also imitate that. This skill is just emerging and is somewhat inconsistent but MUCH better than even 3 to 4 months ago when he didn't even acknowledge other kids were in the park with him!*

We did these imitative drills frequently the first year of therapy. We did imitative play drills every 30 minutes during therapy, and in addition we played with our child directly between every other drill during downtime, redirecting any inappropriate play. We kept a checklist of all downtime activities and tried to do different activities from those done by the person in the previous session. We tried to encourage spontaneous play by placing toys and activities around the room and even changing them after the longer breaks. We rotated toys in and out of the room. All of the toys used during downtime were also targeted in the formal imitative play drills so that they could be generalized and either the tutor or the child could discover new targets.

If I had to do these early play drills over, I would do several things differently. First, I would not have used so many toys. If my child showed an interest in a toy, I would have stuck with that one for a while and really mined it for play and language. Obviously, you have to be aware of perseveration, but typical children carry around the same baby doll until it falls apart and their parents don't take it away from them because they are being rigid. You have to be careful not to confuse comfort and enjoyment of an activity with perseveration and rigidity. Play is supposed to be enjoyable.

Second, I would have been more aware of the normal development of play. This knowledge can help keep you from forcing too advanced play on your child, causing confusion and frustration all around. Figurine play is a good example. Figure 1 (see page 11) demonstrates a rough developmental progression of figurine play. For example, a child might want nothing to do with figurines. Or the child may simply hold a familiar figurine, carry it around, and talk about it ("It's Obi Wan Kenobi!"). Or he or she might want enjoy setting up a scene (i.e., a dollhouse) and moving the figurines into different positions in the scene (scene setup). Or he or she might be able to move a figure (figurine action pretend) and perhaps talk about what the figure is doing (figurine action narration). Your child may even want to act out scenes from movies or books using the figurines, but *still* may not be developmentally ready to move and talk *for* the doll as if the doll could control its own actions and had its own personality (figurine personalities). Some children never do this activity or social figurine play. You have to be aware of these stages in using figurines and other activities so that you can work with where the child is developmentally. Our imitative play targets reflect that we started in using figurines early in our program. While my child eventually played with these items spontaneously (for example, the Fisher-Price Pirate Ship), I believe that we introduced them too early in his program, skipping some more developmentally appropriate (and fun) activities.

Third, I would have used the drills more as a guide in moving to more sophisticated, reciprocal, and spontaneous play rather than as an end unto themselves. Figure 1 (see page 11) shows how a base of imitative targets can lead into all sorts of types of play. As you go away from the basic imitative targets, you are heading into higher and higher developmental areas, and the imitative way of teaching will fade to a more observational and cooperative style. For example, if the child is imitating well doing symbolic pretend play with a doll, I would move that activity into a looser pretend activity, encouraging him or her to add targets and really play rather than keeping the activity as a strict imitative drill. Not all forms of play can be fitted into this model illustrated by Figure 1, but the model does give you an idea of the variety of play and a sense of the hierarchy of play development.

After a few months of single targets in our imitative play program, we did try to loosen up our language and chain the movements, having our child imitate a series of actions, thus simulating more normal play. At this point, our child would start to take the lead and do some of his own actions. This initiative was exciting, but we still made him imitate us for new targets with new activities. When he took the lead, we would follow and try to expand the play as much as possible. We did not originally set out do these drills in this way. Our consultant wanted us to continue to concentrate on imitation only, even after our child was thinking up his own targets. On our own, however, we started using the targets as jumping off places to other skills. Only in retrospect do I see how using this drill's targets in this manner evolved into later forms of play.

USE OF IMITATIVE PLAY TARGETS

You don't have to do every one of these targets (or any of them). I include the list of our imitative play targets just to give you ideas of how to proceed with imitative drills and some mistakes to avoid. It probably is better to concentrate on a few common preschool toys and have many targets for each one rather than buying the toy store. Don't spread your child too thin or he or she will never be comfortable with any single toy. You can have other toys and activities available at any time, but for teaching specific targets, stick with one or two toys at a time. When you get a toy, sit down and play with it and note every step you take to manipulate the toy, no matter how simple. Once you follow this process with a few toys, thinking of targets becomes much easier. If you have another child handy to play with the toy, take notes on what he or she does.

If your child displays no interest in the toy after several attempts, or acts as if the toy is aversive, consider changing to another toy. You can always try to reintroduce the toy later. It is important to know what your child likes. If your child has inappropriate behaviors or obsessions, try to figure out a way to teach him or her an analogous toy or activity that incorporates the obsession. This procedure can convert a lower-level self-stimulatory behavior to a higher-level (and more socially acceptable) one. This conversion is not always possible, however, and if your child persists in playing inappropriately with a toy or object, you may have to remove the object from therapy and reintroduce it at a later date.

Be sure your tutors write down new targets as they are invented. If your child comes up with new actions and verbalizations, be sure to incorporate them into the play with the next tutor! Frequently, the targets listed here were invented during sessions as the tutor or our child spontaneously thought of them. That's why they might look somewhat random, but, in practice, they were chained together in a more sensible fashion than these bare lists suggest.

If your child is in preschool, consider sending a favorite toy to school with him or her. This practice increases tolerance to parallel play and introduces the child to observational learning. Our car garage and dollhouse were popular in kindergarten, and our child, who was familiar with them, was able to play with the other kids, observing and imitating their actions with the toys. As he has grown, I have found that supplying my child with a "cool" toy (like a slip and slide in the front yard) makes neighborhood children much more likely just to show up at our door to play. Their spontaneous participation provides my child with unstructured peer play and further opportunities for observational learning.

Note that these imitative targets can provide your child with a solid base of skills that he or she can expand into more and more sophisticated play. For example, teaching a child the components of activities in a play kitchen leads to social pretend play with peers in a preschool kitchen play center. When you are planning your program, think carefully about how each toy or activity can lead to more complex play. Don't start at the most complex level and try to get the child to work at that level. This leap will only lead to frustration and dead-end programs. Carefully thinking ahead about where a target will lead will also help you avoid teaching targets that have no potential for progressing to more advanced play.

When reviewing these targets, remember that this imitative play program was only *one* of our play programs. We had separate *pretend, manipulative imitation, games,* and *songs* programs all going at the same time as this one. In addition, teaching playskills was only a part of our child's total intervention program that encompassed drills on language, behavior, imitation and observational skills, as well as school skills and academics. Several of these play programs' targets overlapped. In addition to our formal therapy programs, our tutors had to play directly with our child between drills in much less structured activities. Notes were kept on both the formal and informal activities.

Some of our targets went nowhere (for example, felt boards and puppets). Those targets just faded out in therapy. In retrospect, I think this fading out is appropriate. If you can't get the child at all interested, move on to something else.

When you are creating your own targets, remember that it is sometimes very hard for a child to do two things at once. Our first imitative drills involved crashing cars together and saying "Crash" at the same time (which was inappropriate anyway since typical kids just make crashing noises with their mouths when they crash cars together—they don't say "Crash"). Doing an action and verbalizing at the same time proved difficult for my child in the beginning. In your early targets, you might consider sticking with single actions at first without the complexity of verbalization. Verbalizations can be added once the actions are well known.

IMITATIVE PLAY TARGETS

I categorize these targets into separate areas following the outline of this book to demonstrate how imitative targets can be expanded into different types of play. However, this separation and organization of targets was done in retrospect. At the time we did these drills, we just did them in a random way, introducing new toys and targets constantly. We were not aware of the normal development of play and introduced toys and activities that were not always appropriate for my child at the time.

Manipulative Imitation Targets (see Chapter 3)
We first did these targets in manipulative imitation drills and then moved them to imitative play in order to expand the building materials into pretend play.

Duplo Lego Sets
1. Water animals set
2. Race driver
    Put man in race car
    "Shoot" race car
    Tow racecar with tow truck
    Put car in garage
    Have mechanic look at car
3. Playground
4. Indians and teepee
    Put up teepee
    Place Indian in teepee
    Put up fire
    Sit Indians at fire
    Dance at fire
5. Dinosaur park

Blocks
1. Make a tower
2. Make a bed
3. Make a road
4. Make a bridge
5. Make a house
6. Make a house with a chair inside
7. Build a car
8. Have people drive car
9. Crash car
10. Walk people across bridge
11. Put people under bridge
12. Have people slide down end of bridge

Tinker Toys
1. Make a dumbbell
2. Lift weights
3. Make designs
4. Have action figures jump over a design
5. Have the child jump over design

Toobers and Zots
1. Make a crown
2. Wear the crown on head
3. Limbo under toobers
4. Make a hat (cowboy)
5. Make a sword
6. Have a sword fight
7. Put the hat on head
8. Say "yee haw!"
9. Pretend to ride a horse
10. Make and wear a "super powers" belt
11. Make a necklace

Toy Play Target (See Chapter 4)
Many of the closed-end toys that I describe in Chapter 4 were used as reinforcers for my son during therapy. For example, as a reward for doing well in his drills, he got to play with a closed-end toy like a wave bottle or a wind-up toy. We did not have to teach formally those types of toys in his program.

Cars/Garage
1. Crash two cars together (can add crashing noises)
2. Push a car (can add "zooming" noises)
3. Push the car over a ramp (made with blocks)
4. Put gas in the car (gas pump in garage)
5. Park the car in garage

6. Make the car go up the garage elevator
7. Make the car go down the jump ramp (garage)
8. Tow the car with the tow truck
9. Say, "We're going up." (elevator)
10. Say, "Let me off." (elevator)
11. Have the car exit elevator
12. Make the car do donuts
13. Have a little car drive over a big car
14. Make the car do a wheelie
15. Make the car run off the table
16. Have the figurines jump on top of cars
17. Have the police car come to arrest the figurine
18. Put the figurine in jail (make up the jail)

Train Set
1. Lay track down (hook the pieces together)
2. Put the train engine and cars together
3. Move the train over bridge
4. Move the train on the turntable
5. Make train noises (chug a chug, toot-toot)
6. Crash the trains
7. Make a bridge with blocks over track

Drill Truck
1. Change drill bits
2. Drill lug nuts on tires
3. Do wheelie
4. Take truck apart with drill

Large Crane/Construction Set
1. Have people climb the crane
2. Have people fall down inside
3. Rescue people
4. Raise the elevator (with button)
5. Put up crane (hook)
6. Have men walk along the top
7. Have figures board the elevator
8. Have figures exit the elevator
9. Have figures ride the truck to lunch
10. Have a person jump off crane
11. Hook up lift/platform to crane
12. Say "Lift 'er up."
13. Say "Time for lunch."
14. Say "Good crew here."

Dump truck

1. Load (with anything)
2. Dump the load out
3. Drive the truck around
4. Make truck noises
5. Back up truck
6. Make "beep noise" for reversing
7. Say "Thanks for the delivery."
8. Put men in the truck (back)
9. Make the truck roll over hills (rug wrinkles)
10. Make people fall out of the dump truck

Vehicles Large

1. Crash trucks
2. Run over people
3. Jump ramp (made from blocks)

Panama Canal/Boats

1. Pump water
2. Push boats
3. Crash boats
4. Use the crane to lift out boats
5. Release water from central lock

In-Vivo Pretend Targets (See Chapter 5)

These targets are easy to expand into the pretend activities discussed in chapter 5. Many of our dress up and pretend scenarios originated with these imitative targets.

Baby Dolls

1. Hug doll
2. Comb doll's hair
3. Pretend feed doll (spoon)
4. Kiss doll
5. Rock doll
6. Cover doll with blanket
7. Put a shirt on the doll
8. Put the doll in the crib
9. Pat the baby on the back (over shoulder...like burping)
10. Put a diaper on the doll
11. Put pants on the doll
12. Feed the baby with a bottle

Doctor's Kit

1. Put on a Band-Aid
2. Take temperature

3. Give a shot
4. Use a doll as patient
5. Listen to the heart with stethoscope
6. Put a cast on the doll's leg
7. Take the doll's blood pressure
8. Have the tutor be a patient

Play Food/Kitchen
1. "Eat" toy food
2. "Pour" tea (or coffee)
3. Put play food on plates
4. Set place setting/table
5. Eat with utensils
6. Cut food
7. Cook food on a stove (use different pots and pans)
8. Cook food in an oven
9. Cook food in the microwave
10. Wash dishes in the sink
11. Put food in the refrigerator
12. Serve food to the table
13. Put away dishes

Tool Bench
1. Hammer nail
2. Screw in bolt-screwdriver
3. Unscrew bolt-screwdriver
4. Screw in bolt-wrench
5. Unscrew bolt-wrench
6. Put square in vise
7. Put on belt and put tools in the belt
8. Measure with the measuring tape
9. Wash hands in sink
10. Turn on the radio
11. Answer the phone
12. Pull out a nail with pliers

Camping Set/Tent
1. Pretend (with flashlight) to be looking through the woods
2. Drink from the canteen
3. Eat with a fork and pan
4. Make a fire (with blocks)
5. Cook food over the campfire
6. Pour water into a cup
7. Eat food out of a bowl
8. Say "Foods ready!"
9. Say "That's delicious!"
10. Say "Mmm—I was thirsty."
11. Drink from a cup
12. Say "Ooh it's spooky and dark."

Dress Up
Ambulance Driver
1. Put on hat and coat
2. Drive the ambulance (chairs as ambulance)
3. Make siren sounds
4. Find a sick person (doll)
5. Give CPR (push chest, blow on mouth)
6. Put the doll in ambulance

Cash Register
Have cashier:
1. Say "What would you like?"
2. Say "That will be $____."
3. Give shopper desired object
4. Say "cash or charge?"
5. Say "Thank you—have a nice day."

Have shopper:
1. Say "I want to buy _____."
2. Put things to buy on the counter
3. Say "Thank you."

In Vitro Pretend (See Chapter 6)
Many of our imitative in vitro targets concentrated on playset arrangements and figurine action pretend. However, our child was not ready for figurine narration at the time we worked on these targets.

Maisy Dollhouse
1. Put Maisy in the bathtub
2. Brush Maisy with a brush
3. Put clothes on Maisy
4. Put Maisy in the bed
5. Give Maisy OJ
6. Make Maisy look in the cupboard
7. Make Maisy hang up clothes in the closet

Pirate ship—Fisher-Price
1. "Sail" the ship
2. Steer the ship...man at helm
3. Shoot a cannonball— say "boom"
4. Shoot the harpoon
5. Put a man in the crow's nest
6. Row a dinghy to the island
7. Shoot a cannonball from an island tree
8. Put a pirate in jail on the island
9. Put the treasure chest in the dinghy
10. Drop anchor
11. Shoot the harpoon at whale
12. Say "Man overboard" and have a man fall off
13. Have a shark attack the dinghy
14. Put men on sails (they snap on)

Figurines
1. "Walk" figures
2. Have the dog run and bark
3. Have the dog lick the face
4. Have figurines run across the table
5. Have a figure jump off diving board into pool (manipulative imitation)
6. Say "Splash!"

Submarine-Fisher-Price
1. Put a figure inside sub
2. Have the figure look through periscope
3. Spin the propeller
4. Shoot torpedoes
5. Push around the sub (as if it were under water)
6. Have a figure dive off the sub
7. Make an octopus attack the man
8. Have the shark eat the figure
9. Drill into mountains/hills with sub drill
10. Sing "Kokomo"

11. Make the octopus attack Goldfish crackers
12. Make splashing noises
13. Have a figure climb the sub
14. Put on the door
15. Hook a figure on the hook
16. Raise the figure from the water

Western Town—Fisher-Price
1. Put figure on a horse
2. Make the horse gallop
3. Put the figure in jail and close jail door
4. Walk the figure up side stairs
5. Catapult a man off the top of the roof
6. Pull the flag backwards and slide the man down chute
7. Say "Giddy up" and push the stagecoach forward
8. Say "Whoa..." and stop the stagecoach
9. Fire the stagecoach cannon
10. Make the figure fall off of the trick staircase
11. Make the horse drink at trough

Dinosaurs
1. Have the dinosaurs climb on each other
2. Have the dinosaurs eat trees
3. Make roaring noises
4. Have the dinosaur fly (the pterodactyl)
5. Have the dinosaur make noises while it is flying ("wok wok")

Castle—Fisher Price
1. Have a figure climb the wall (with foot holes)
2. Make the figure fall or jump off the top
3. Have the barbarian/giant knock on the castle
4. Raise/lower the drawbridge
5. Make a figure fall down the trap
6. Shoot the cannon
7. Use the battering ram to ram castle
8. Put a figure on the battering ram
9. Put up the table
10. Have a figure walk on the inside ledge
11. Rescue figures (secret door on side)
12. Have figures sleep in the bed
13. Have the barbarian say: "I want food"

Wood Dollhouse
1. Set up kitchen
2. Set up living room
3. Set up bedroom
4. Set up bathroom
5. Put a doll at kitchen table
6. Have the doll wash face
7. Have the doll go to bed
8. Have the doll sit on the potty
9. Have the doll take a bath
10. Have the doll climb up the rope ladder
11. Have the dolls sit in chairs
12. Have the dolls slide down the slide
13. Have the doll swing
14. Place the dolls on the see-saw
15. Plant a garden

Physical and Sensory Play Targets (See Chapter 9)
Many of these activities were performed informally during unstructured playtime with the tutors.

Sockem Bopem
1. Put boppers on hands
2. Fight with the tutor (hitting bopper only)
3. Pretend to hit self in head and fall down
4. Hit the fish on the mat
5. Pretend to be a pumpkin (put boppers on top of your head)
6. Punch forward (not side-armed)

Dances
1. Hokey Pokey
2. Bunny Hop
3. Freeze dance

Gymnastics
1. Do a forward roll
2. Walk on balance beam (pretend)

Playdough
1. Make a snake (noodle)
2. Roll a ball
3. Make a "pancake"
4. Make a hot dog (one flat piece, one rolled piece, put together)
5. Make a snowman
6. Use cookie cutters
7. Make a bracelet
8. Make a hamburger (three flat pieces with different colors for beef and bread)
9. Make spaghetti (thinner noodles)
10. Make a clown (eyes, hair, nose) face only
11. Use a rolling pin
12. Make a donut

Wrestling
Use stuffed animals or dolls
1. Clothes line
2. Elbow drop
3. Raise the roof
4. "The rack"

Sword Fighting
1. Hit swords together (no hitting the other person!)
2. Practice knocking the sword out of the other person's hand

Less Successful Targets
These targets were introduced in therapy but did not progress very far. My child enjoyed playing with some of them, for example, the Colorforms and the Magi-Cloth theater, but we did not spend a great deal of time teaching him specific things to do. Others, such as puppets, he disliked.

Colorforms
1. Spiderman
2. Batman
3. Blue's Clues

Magi-Cloth Theater
1. Arthur
2. Busytown

Puppets
1. Open mouth
2. Close the hands (clapping)
3. Nod the head

Felt Boards and People
1. Put one item on the board
2. Put a person on the board
3. Put a person on the board and put on clothes

Potato Heads

Lincoln Logs

Swing Set
1. Swing legs out
2. Swing legs in
3. Pump arms
4. Lean back
5. Slide
6. Hang by knees on trapeze
7. Train on slide with the child in front and tutor in back (say "Choo choo")

Star Wars Set
1. Walk Yoda across bridge
2. Have a figure fall in the hole
3. Put up the tree
4. Have figure climb the tree

Blues Clues
1. Draw a clue
2. Look for a clue

Winnie the Pooh Play Set—Western
1. Walk to the door
2. Knock on the door
3. Say "Is anybody home?"
4. Grab a figure and put it in jail
5. Say "Oh, no, I've been captured!"

INDEPENDENT PLAY

After our child had learned many imitative drill targets, we tried to teach him to play independently with his known toys and activities. In this drill, my child was asked to play alone with toys the tutors had chosen. The tutors timed how long he could play with the toy independently without their interference. I don't think that this independent play drill was particularly effective for my child during his early play. In retrospect, he progressed much faster by learning play from interactions with a tutor or another child. He wanted the tutors to play with him and being left alone to play, particularly with toys he didn't especially care for, frustrated him. Now, he can and does play independently with self-chosen activities, but I believe we pushed this activity in therapy too soon. We did this drill for only about four months before we moved on to other types of play activities. After a couple of months, we decided to let him pick the activity, and we intervened only if he was playing inappropriately. Then we stopped just telling him to "Go play with _____" and started each activity as a cooperative one (tutor and child playing together). We played for a while with him and then faded ourselves out and monitored his independent play. The following tutor notes excerpted from the data on this drill show how we slowly changed the format of this drill from strictly making him do what we wanted him to to allowing him to choose the toy to finally playing with him using toys and activities chosen by either him or his tutor. The notes also reflect when the tutors began to play cooperatively with him and how that interaction improved the experience. The notes also point out some of the difficulties of doing this drill too soon (noncompliance, lack of interest, and inappropriate play).

TUTOR NOTES—INDEPENDENT PLAY DRILL

He played with the wooden vehicle puzzles. Excellent job. Worked for 4 minutes.

I gave Eric the blocks and the manipulative imitation pictures. He played great by himself. He built a few different structures. He then played with the Western Town and the Pirate Ship appropriately.

Played with Playdoh, Pirate Ship and Western Town. He had some of the figures talk to each other.

Played with the Pirate Ship. He put the pirates in jail. He saw crabs in the sand and sharks in the water.

He played independently with Thomas the Tank Engine tracks and engines for about 3-4 minutes.

I had him string beads. I had to fully physically prompt him and also use a lot of verbal prompts. Once he got started, he did a great job and I got a beautiful necklace.

Car Garage. He perseverated on the spiral ramp. I verbally prompted him to do something else with no success. I went to nonverbal imitation with some success but he continued to do the same action when I left to let him play independently. He needs help on this drill.

Duplo Water Animals. He built a pool and had the whale swim in the pool.

Barbies. He played OK. He said they were going to the pool. Then he put them in the car. At the end, he

took them to the dollhouse. He wasn't really into it much. I will try a different activity next time.
Dollhouse. Played for 3 minutes. I gave several prompts for ideas. Eric was slow getting started, then I prompted to put the doll to bed. Then after a few seconds, I prompted him to make breakfast and then again prompted him to put the doll in the tub. He is not ready to move on with independent play.

Baby Dolls. Pretty good! Started to dress the doll. He wanted a blanket to put over the baby, etc. He kept repeating words and actions until I acknowledged him. I tried to keep myself out of it as much as possible.

Baby Dolls. At first, he wanted me to play with him, but I told him that I wanted him to play by himself because I had to "write." He started by rocking the babies and then began to dress them.

Potato Heads. He played about 2 minutes. He was not very interested. He said, "Nope, I'm going to pick them up." He put them up, but got out the Duplo car and wrecker set on his own and asked if he could play with it. I timed him for three minutes. Great play! Should we let him pick his own toy to play with?

Large Cardboard Blocks. We started to build a house for gorilla and teddy bear. I faded myself out after the "earthquake" and he rebuilt the house for them and played for 2 minutes by himself.

Legos. It took a few minutes for him to play with them. He had a very hard time starting, so I had to sit with him, then fade. He did great afterward. He built a car and said, "Wait for me" and "They're driving."

Car Garage. Good! Four verbal prompts (3 to do something else; 1 for encouragement). Actions included pushing cards down the spiral ramp, moving cars up the elevator and down the ramp, raising the top lever of the red ramp and placing the cards against it. He then dropped the lever for the cards to drop. He repeated several of these actions, but not sequentially (they were interspersed with other activities)

Crane. 3 minutes. Played pretty well with it. Had to keep giving him prompts to keep playing. He sang his ABCs while he played with it.

Dollhouse. He kept putting the doll to bed and saying, "She's sleeping." Needed prompting to make her do something else. He did not play for the full three minutes.

Dollhouse. Was not interested. He wanted to play with the bus. He needed full verbal prompting for the entire two minutes.

Duplo Wrecker Set. Played for 5 minutes. Good play. He said what he was doing and said, "Watch this."

Workbench. Took him about 1 1/2 minutes to warm-up with several prompts. Once he got started, he had no problem. He used the screwdriver, mallet, measuring tape, and washed his hands.

Pirate Ship. Total noncompliance. After behavioral intervention, he said wanted to play with the ship. Good play for three minutes.

Duplos. After I played with him for one minute, he played great alone. He built a tall car for the people and drove it around the room.

Drill Crane Set. Very interested in drilling and taking it apart and putting it back together. Needed no prompts.

Workbench. I put the tool belt on him. Then I prompted him through most of the actions. He wanted to be a police officer. I showed him some new things about the workbench by imitation.

Wooden Blocks. We built a sandcastle together. Then I left and he built a house. He likes to knock the structures down. 4 minutes.

Tinker Toys. He asked for them, so I let have them for this program. He built a helicopter and other unnamed structures. 3 minutes.

Potato Heads. He went and got them himself and said, "I want to play Hot Potato."

Dollhouse. He wanted to play with it, so I took advantage of that. I prompted him to give the doll a bath and what parts to wash to get him started. He did not self- narrate but played appropriate actions.

Drill Truck and Crane Set. He played great with the set for 5 minutes, then we did another drill, and then he played for about 3 minutes more. He was very happy playing, singing, and drilling. Great playtime.

Dollhouse. I began with doing imitative play, then I backed out. Eric played appropriately for 2-3 minutes, then dumped the house over. I made him clean it up and we did another drill.

Train Set. He played for 4 minutes, identifying the trains and talking about them as he arranged them on the track. He was completely independent and I only instructed him to "Go play with the Trains."

Western Town. Great playing for 5 minutes. He set up the stagecoach with horses and men and then shot cannon. He made voices for the people!

Pirate Ship. I started playing with him and then faded out. He perseverated on the anchor string and tied up the pirate with it.

Western Town. I used the red timer to give him a visual prompt. He incorporated Mom into his play. Played great for about 3 minutes.

Legos. It started out as an imitative drill, then I faded out and Eric played well and built structures for 4 minutes afterwards.

Western Town. Good playing. Put men on horse. Put men into the carriage and crashed it into the town buildings. 3 minutes. Then I played with him for some imitative play.

Kitchen. He started with the kitchen (cook dinner, eat, put away) but then gathered up some items and asked, "Will you beep?" (The kids play grocery store at school. The kids are usually shoppers and a teacher is the cashier. The cashier takes the item from the child and slides it across the "scanner" on the table and says, "beep" while doing so). The kitchen play looked great but only lasted approximately 3 minutes. I didn't want to discourage his coming up with the grocery store idea so I participated. We did the grocery store routine three times, but each time he "bought" different items.

Car Garage and Racetrack. Great playing. We put the raceway together and then he put the cars on it. We did a countdown for each car: "1,2,3, go."

Tea Party. His brother set up a nice table for us and served us both. Eric behaved like a gentleman and ordered off of the "menu."

Car Garage and Track. We build the road and then Eric played with it on several occasions (during the therapy session). He drove cars up and down the ramp, took them to the mechanic and put up streetlights.

Wooden Blocks. I asked him to build a house with a chimney. He built a large structure for 3 minutes. He knocked it down, then cleaned up and got another toy.

Castle. I tried independent play, but he kept stuffing knights down the tower. I turned it into cooperative play and we played for 8 minutes.

Construction Crane. Wound the figure up in the crane string. I made him stop and move on to something else.

Castle. I played cooperatively with him. Looked pretty good. I faded out after about 5 minutes and he maintained appropriate play for about 3 minutes more (appropriate = anything but stuffing the knights down the tower). After about three minutes, he began stuffing the knights again.

Kitchen. Completely independent. 10 minutes. He made a grand meal. Narrated with some of the functions (cook on the stove, cook in the oven, cook with the pot, etc.)

Felt Board. Played appropriately for about 2 minutes, then began to play inappropriately with the felt pieces (rummaging through the box, but not picking out anything.)

Arthur's Playset. 3 minutes. Played well for about 2 minutes and then started piling objects into a hat and asking me random questions. He needed prompting to get Arthur out and take him to school.

Arthur's Playset. I began to play with Eric and then faded out. He made a school bus out of my shoes and pretended the dollhouse was a school. He took them swimming too. Great imagination. Actual independent play alone was 5 minutes.

Independent Play. 10 minutes
I set out Legos, Felt, Submarine, Etch-a-Sketch, and Camping Gear.
Camping gear. He played inappropriately with the lantern and binoculars.
Etch-a-Sketch. Ignored it.

Submarine. Opened and closed the door. Tilted sub back and forth to watch the man inside fall from one end to the other.

Felt. Took pieces out and put them back in.

Legos. Kept building with the same size block in an ABAB alternating color pattern.

Cooperative Play. 10 minutes

Same options as independent play.

Camping gear. Got Eric decked out in the gear and we went "camping." Went to the corner of the room to a book with animals on the cover. We were "scared" of the animals and ran away. He opened a large hard cover book and set it up as a "tent." Then we went to sleep.

Felt/Submarine. We made an ocean scene and the submarine shot the felt submarine. Divers swam over, caught fish, and put them into the sub. We put the divers back into the submarine and sailed away.

Legos. We made a school. Eric continued to build in the same color or ABAB alternating patters.
There was very little participation from Eric. He was not motivated.

Puzzle. We worked for 15 minutes together, and then Eric worked independently for 5 minutes to finish it.

Magi-Cloth Theater. He chose the Richard Scarry figures. He asked a lot of questions and played very well. He went to the other room to ask his brother the name of one of the characters.

Chapter 3
Manipulatives and Building

- *Wooden Blocks*
- *Duplos*
- *Legomania*
- *Other Building Materials*

Manipulative imitation drills teach the child to manipulate construction materials initially via imitation, and then they teach the child to build novel structures independently. Ultimately, the child learns to build a structure as a common goal in a peer-play situation, modifying his or her own building techniques and ideas via observational learning.

Once your child learns to use a few different materials, manipulative play may be expanded and incorporated into other forms of play. For example, the child may build an entire scene using multiple materials such as a city built with blocks and Duplos. Figurines and embellishments may then be added (other manipulative structures and vehicles, cars, people, animals, trees, and signs) so that the entire creation can be used for further toy and figurine play.

WOODEN BLOCKS

Start teaching manipulative imitation with a set of large, plain wooden blocks of various shapes and sizes and perhaps a set of colored wooden blocks as well. Blocks are the most common manipulative used in preschool and are easy for little hands to handle. Specific teaching techniques and reinforcement will depend on your program, but a general program progression is as follows.

First, the child imitates *abstract block structures* one block at a time as the tutor builds them. The tutor says, "Do this" or a variation, and places a single block from his or her own set of blocks. The child copies the tutor's actions with a block from his or her own set. This drill begins with just two blocks and progresses to structures with up to ten or so blocks. At the beginning, the child should have only the appropriate blocks available, and they should be supplied to him or her one at a time. The emphasis here is on the child's correctly placing his or her block by imitating the tutor's structure. Later, the tutor raises the difficulty by giving the child an increasing numbers of blocks to choose from until the child is faced with a box of blocks to look through to pick each appropriate block for the structure. When the child can copy novel abstract structures of ten blocks without hesitation, then he or she can progress to copying completed structures. In this case, the child does not watch and build at the same time as the tutor, but builds only after the tutor completes the building. The tutor builds the structure and shows it to the child, asking him or her to "Build this." As the child progresses, a photograph of a completed abstract structure may be used. The child must figure out how to build the structure by looking at the completed example and using spatial and temporal sequencing.

Next, the child is asked to build *specific, identifiable structures*. Depending on the child, this step can be done by having the tutor either model the structure or by using photographs of completed structures. The child is presented with an example of a completed structure or a picture and asked to "Build this _____." Consider using several different examples for each object, for example, several different bridges or houses so that the child is exposed to different ways of building the same thing. We frequently used the completed structures for imitative play drills and pretend. That is, we actually played with the structures after they were built. Of course, we always worked on language by identifying the structure and talking about it if possible. We incorporated questions and prompted comments that related to other concepts the child was working on elsewhere in therapy. For example we might ask, "Where's the big red block?" or "Show me the top of the tower." We might also comment on an event: "Oh NO! What happened? It fell down!"

Once the child can build the actual structures easily with the picture, the picture is faded out by shorter and shorter presentations of the picture prior to the child's building. Eventually, the child is asked to build the structure from memory. For example, you might say, "Build a tree." Finally, the child is given novel blocks and asked to generalize the known structures by building with different blocks and different styles. In practice, we had four different houses that our child built using pictures so that by the time we got to this step, our child had already learned that there is more than one way to build a house.

Finally, the child is asked to build *novel structures* such as a castle, table, barn, car garage, or steamroller. If at any point during the teaching of blocks the child builds novel structures on his or her own, that creativity should be reinforced. If the child has learned and demonstrated solid imitation skills, then once he or she begins self-initiated building, the tutor should be able to switch gears, stop forcing imitation of the pre-set targets, and begin to follow the child creating more cooperative and interactive play. This transition can be hard to identify and accomplish. There is a definite need to teach solid imitation skills, but the final goal of teaching manipulatives is to allow the child to build on his or her own and to participate in cooperative group building.

[Tutor note] *After generalizing some known structures with different blocks, I asked him to build an 18-wheeler (novel structure). It was cool! He used 3 sets of wheels, a cab, and a trailer.*

DUPLOS—THE LARGE LEGOS

These large Legos are also a common manipulative material found in preschools. They are not as flexible for building structures as the wooden blocks, but they do provide practice for playing with the smaller Legos and help develop fine motor skills. The first step in teaching manipulative imitation with Duplos is the same as with wooden blocks. However, you don't have to start over at this point. By this time, the child should be easily able to imitate building with manipulatives. You need to show the child how to manipulate the Duplo pieces—how to put them together and pull them apart. After the child can work with the pieces fairly easily, move quickly though some abstract structures and then some actual structures. You can also use photographs for these targets as well.

Next, introduce the boxed Duplo sets that are available. Put these together using the pictures on the boxes as a guide. There are usually two or three ways you can arrange the pieces, so try the different ones, using

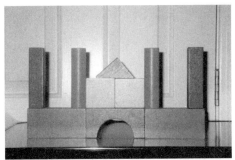

10 Blocks

Bed 1

Bed 2

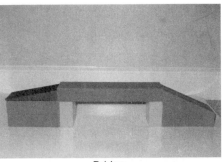

Bridge

Car

Chair with Lamp

Chair

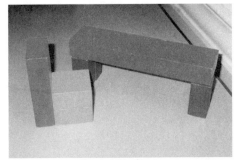

Desk with Chair

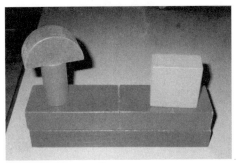

Dresser

House 1

House 2

House 2 Side

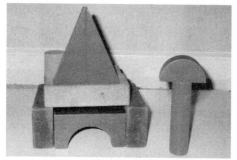

House 3

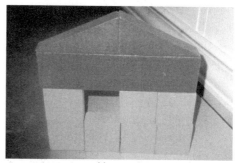

House 4

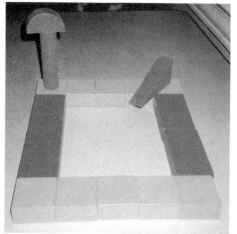

Pool

Sailboat

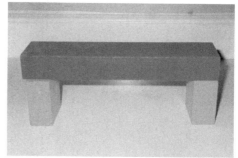

Simple Bridge

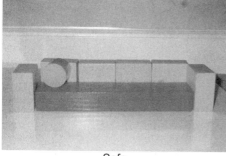

Sofa

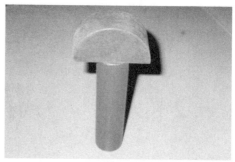

Tree

the pictures on the box as a guide. After you set up a scene, then you can play with the pieces and figurines, using imitative play drill techniques and progressing to pretend play. Examples of available Duplo playsets include:

➢ Water animals
➢ Race car drivers
➢ Native Americans
➢ Prehistoric park
➢ Playground

[Tutor note] *We built the Duplo playground and played school. We pretended the Duplo Indians were kids at school. They played on the playground, did a circle time, got in a car, and went home.*

LEGOS

Building with the regular Legos by following the printed instructions is a natural progression from the manipulative imitation drills. Lego play provides an activity that both of my children enjoy and can play together. My older child likes to create novel structures and play imaginatively with them. Not surprisingly, my ASD child has a more "engineering" approach to the materials. He likes to follow the instructions exactly as written and create the structure as designed. We are teaching him to incorporate flexibility into his designs, to play creatively with the completed structures, and to produce novel structures.

Before you introduce Legos to your child, make sure he or she has the *fine motor skills* to manipulate most of the pieces. We did not start Legos until our child was six years old. The child should be able to manipulate Duplos (the big Legos) without difficulty before trying the little ones. For some time, however, you will still have to manipulate the little bitty ones for the child.

With any activity such as Legos that involves many small pieces, it is critical to be *organized*! I strongly believe that no child can play with disorganized materials, especially with toys that have a gazillion little pieces. Any child will become overwhelmed with all the mess and space out. When we first started building with Legos, I tried to keep the individual Lego sets separate, each with its own instructions in a container, but this organizational attempt proved futile. The best solution I have come up with is just to sort out all the pieces by color after your initial set-build and breakdown. Use plastic containers (dishpans are good and you can stack them). Put all the instruction manuals together in another container. The very tiny and unusual pieces are all put together in yet another container. In this system, all the pieces from the various sets will be mixed up, but this mixture can actually be useful in teaching flexibility (once you can convince your child to use a piece that has the same shape as the one in the drawing, but a different color). When you come across random pieces that you will inevitably find in the sofa or under your bare feet, you can just throw them into the appropriate container.

In beginning Lego play, *put the sets together first yourself.* When starting on your first sets, you will save yourself and your child a lot of time and trouble if you do this initial construction yourself (without the child present). This pre-construction is necessary in the beginning of Lego play because frequently the building directions require very good spatial-perspective skills and you may have to take some time to figure out how the pieces should be oriented. You don't want to have to do this in the middle of teaching. Later, when you and your child are more proficient, you can just open the box and go.

Be sure to *introduce small sets first*. A simple car is usually manageable and can be played with easily after construction. These early small sets usually have only a few pieces and less than ten instructional steps. Place all the parts on the work surface and show the child the instruction sheet. Point to the first instruction picture, generally labeled "1." Tell the child that this picture is first, and ask the child to find the pieces needed for the picture and to make a structure that matches the picture (use whatever language works for your child). The newer Lego set instructions have an inset box that shows all the pieces needed for a particular step on the same page as the picture of the structure. With these instructions, the child can gather up all the pieces needed for the step, then look at the picture to see where they are placed. The older Lego set instructions do not have this inset box and the child has to look at each picture to figure out what pieces are needed to complete the instructional step. Help the child find, orient, and place the pieces. Before moving to the next step, have the child compare his structure to the picture to make sure that he or she has completed all the steps for that instruction.

Usually I say something like, "Here's the number 1. This is the first picture. What pieces do we need? Can you put them together like this picture? Does that look right? Are we finished with this picture? What's the next step? Here's the number 2. It's the second (or next) picture. What do we need now? Can you find the pieces?" Continue in this manner until the creation is finished. You can work on numbers and sequencing in addition to visual imitation and fine motor skills. Keep these early sets separated into a zip lock bag containing all the pieces and instructions.

Do the small piece several times with the child, and then see if the child can do it independently. Our child built a small jeep at least ten or fifteen times on his own before he spontaneously moved to bigger sets. If your child is interested in a particular Lego theme, then you can do a several related sets. Legos regularly introduces new themes with multiple related sets. These themes include *Star Wars*, Soccer, Arctic, Knights Kingdom, Life on Mars, Explorers, Lego Studio kits, trains and various vehicles. We did almost every single *Star Wars* Lego set over the course of several months. By that point, we were then able to talk about them and play with them. For example, we built the *Phantom Menace* podracers and ran around the house racing them. We built the Gungan submarine and pretended to be the sea monsters eating it. We regularly rebuild old favorites and leave them together so that they can be played with.

> **[Tutor note]** *I helped him put together the Star Wars Podracer. He showed me which pieces he needed and after a prompt asked me to help him look for them. After we built the podracer, he pretended his figure (Annakin) was fighting my figure (Darth Maul). Good language throughout. He told me he wanted to attack and then he said his light saber broke.*

Searching for an appropriate piece in a large bin of same color pieces is very difficult. Due to this difficulty, my child would not look for pieces and demanded that the adult find the pieces for him. We approached this problem two ways. First, we made him give us a good description of the piece before we would find it for him ("It's a dark gray, flat, 8-dot piece"). Second, we would find the piece, but put it into a small pile of distracter pieces. He still had to scan these pieces to find the correct one, but the handful that he had to look through was a feasible number for him. You might consider doing the following "rummage" drill with your child to teach him or her to look for a specific item in a box full of objects without dumping the entire box contents on the floor. Place two items in a box. Then ask the child to select the correct item and remove it from the box. This drill is easier to do if the child desires the chosen item. For example, put a pencil and a piece of candy in the box and ask the child to pick out the candy. The number of items is increased until the child can "rummage" through a box full of items (without dumping the contents of the box) to find the desired one. This "rummage" drill may help the child, but since finding Lego pieces is difficult for everyone, you will probably need to assist him or her for some time.

Our son didn't care for Legos at age 4.5. They were boring to him because our tutors were making houses and beds with them and he had a fine motor delay that made the Legos hard for him to manipulate. He got more into it at age 5 when we bought the cheap sets that built machines or boats. When we used them to build engine sheds, garages, and Pokemon boxes, Legos were seen to be more exciting. Now that he is almost 6, he does play with Legos. He really got into them more when we hired a male tutor. Additionally, we joined the free Lego Kids' Club to get that hokey magazine. Our son would get play ideas from the magazine. His fine motor skills are better and he builds what he wants and not what the tutor wants. We simply should have waited till he had better fine motor ability for Legos or in the very least, not made boring things out of them.

OTHER BUILDING MATERIALS

Other common preschool manipulatives and building materials include:

➢ Big cardboard blocks—these are commonly found in preschool centers
➢ Brio Building System—these sets use plastic tools and bolts
➢ Beads—large and small for lacing and stringing
➢ Cardboard boxes (for building large items such as houses and castles)

Stick with the basic preschool manipulatives for a long time. If your child develops a further interest in building, then you can progress to some of the harder and more complicated materials. Some of these materials are very complex, however, and are designed for older children. Remember that your child's peers may not be able to play with these materials, so be careful about introducing them in playdate situations if you are not sure about the peer's building interests and ability.

➢ Tinker Toys
➢ Lincoln Logs
➢ Lego Dacto and Technic
➢ Rokenbok Factory
➢ K'Nex
➢ Gear Factory
➢ Pony Beads

Chapter 4
Toy Play

- *Closed-End Toys*
- *Puzzles*
- *Construction Toys*
- *Open-End Toys and Vehicles*

CLOSED-END TOYS

I call some toys *closed-end* because they have a definite beginning or end (for example, a puzzle) or they have a limited number of motions or activities associated with them. These are generally the exploratory toys designed for very young children and babies. You need to show your child how to manipulate these toys correctly yet preserve the exploratory aspect of them—it is a delicate balance.

You do have to be aware that your child might play repetitively with closed-end toys. Since many of these toys are actually designed for repetitive type play, you should be prepared to observe your child and intervene if he or she plays inappropriately with the toy. You may be able to teach your child to play with an appropriate toy that has effects and actions analogous to his or her self-stimulatory behavior. In doing this teaching, you might be able to elevate the level of your child's repetitive self-stimulatory behavior from something that is very inappropriate to something that is more appropriate.

For example, if your child holds objects up to his or her eye to look at them, having him or her hold a kaleidoscope up to his eye and looking into it is more appropriate than squinting at random objects, and yet it still fulfills whatever need the child has for the visual stimulation. You will need to monitor the child for persistent activity beyond what is appropriate. The appropriate duration of time for each activity, however, is sometimes hard to judge. Observations of typical peers doing the same activities may help guide you.

If you have a variety of closed-end toys, you can limit the time with each one, avoiding prolonged repetitive behavior with any single one. You can also demonstrate to the child the many different things that might occur, for example, with the pushing of a button or holding a visual toy in various ways. You can temporarily withdraw a toy if the child will manipulate it only inappropriately and continue to let him or her play with it only if the child handles it correctly—although in early play, I would be fairly lenient in the definition of *correctly*.

On the other hand, I don't think you have to buy lots and lots of these toys. If your child understands how to manipulate a few of them, let him or her explore using them and then move on to somewhat more structured activities. It is important, however, to allow the child the time just to explore some with these kinds of toys before moving on to more structured activities. This is the type of exploration and repetitive motion that babies and young toddlers do, and your child might have missed this opportunity for random exploration as a result of his or her developmental delay.

My child liked the visual type of closed-end toys like kaleidoscopes, wave bottles, tornado bottles, lava lamps, and bubbles. Your child might like the auditory or tactile ones. Have the child explore a variety of different kinds of toys to learn what types of things he or she likes. When you notice some patterns in what the child likes, take note of it and brainstorm about how you can use those preferences in later play.

Unfortunately, this use of the child's preferences may prove impossible for some things. For example, my child liked to get two Barbie dolls and wet their hair. Then, he would hold one in each hand and shake them back and forth, watching the water fly. This was clearly inappropriate behavior. Although he could do a few appropriate things with the dolls, such as acting out some short scenes from movies, I still removed the dolls from the house and worked on other goals. I could not let him play with the Barbies without his sneaking off to wet their hair. An alternative to removing the dolls completely would have been to let him play with them only under supervision. This alternative requires locking up the toys, though, and that can be impractical if you have more than one child.

To teach the manipulation of these toys, start with having the child imitate your behavior. At times, this activity might require having two identical toys, one for the tutor and one for the student. You might not be able to hold up a toy and do something with it and then hand it to the child and have him or her do it. The delay might be too long for the child. Other toys, like an action board, can be played together with the child. Be sure to imitate the child if he or she does something appropriate with the toy.

Examples of Closed-End Toys
➢ Toys that pop up, make noises, fly around, or light up
➢ Electronic toys in general and battery operated toys
➢ Exploratory baby board toys that have several activities like pushing buttons, dialing a dial, looking at a mirror, and sliding doors
➢ Sit and spin
➢ Shape sorters
➢ Punching balls
➢ Ring stackers and nesting cups
➢ Pop-up toys
➢ Pinwheels
➢ Wind-up toys
➢ Jack in the boxes
➢ Sound books
➢ Light swords
➢ Ball games where you hit a ball and it goes down a chute or shaft
➢ Car simulation/steering wheel devices that allow the child to "drive" the car by turning a wheel and honking the horn
➢ Bubble makers that the child can manipulate
➢ Punching dolls—the old-fashioned kind that the child can knock down and then pop back up

- Kaleidoscopes, wave bottles, lava lamps, bubble bottles, tornado bottles, snow globes, glitter wands
- Horns, bells, drums, keyboards and other musical toys
- Viewmaster
- Flashlights of various sizes
- Bumble Ball
- Giant bead maze
- Flip books
- Spinning tops that spin, light up or play music
- Rain Stick
- Stickers and self inking rubber stamps
- Pull string helicopters
- Whistles
- Music box
- Stomp rockets
- Slinky
- Marble maze
- Silly string
- Pom poms
- Clappers
- Lite Bright

Some simple visual closed-end toys that you can make at home include:

Sparkle Bottle. Kids love these. Fill a small, clear, plastic soda bottle three-fourths full with light corn syrup. Add a handful of metallic confetti. Top the bottle off with water and add food coloring as desired. Seal the bottle with the cap and shake to distribute the confetti.

Wave Bottles. A wave bottle creates waves of water over a layer of oil. To make a wave bottle fill a clear, plastic bottle (at least 10 inches high) three-fourths full using denatured alcohol. Add blue food coloring if desired. Fill the bottle with vegetable oil, leaving a small space at the top. Seal with the cap and glue the top on for added safety. A simpler recipe for a wave bottle requires only oil and water. Fill a large, clear, plastic soda bottle half way with water. Add food color if desired. Fill the rest of the bottle with vegetable oil, leaving a small space at the top.

The movement of the water in a wave bottle is fascinating. Swirl the wave bottle while it's standing up or lay it down on its side and rock it back and forth to create waves. Try creating large bubbles by turning the bottle top over bottom a few times. Shake it vigorously to create millions of tiny bubbles

PUZZLES

Like any other sort of play, puzzles have to be reinforcing to your child. Be sure to get puzzle themes that interest your child. Don't buy puzzles that concern things he or she doesn't like or care about. If your child loves Winnie the Pooh, then he or she is more likely to want to put together a Winnie the Pooh puzzle than a Barney puzzle. I would avoid educational puzzles in early play. You want the child to enjoy putting the puzzle together for the reward of seeing this creation made and seeing a picture of interest to him or her.

Puzzles have a progression of difficulty. Start with simple inset puzzles that are noninterlocking, with or without knobs. You can lay the piece just adjacent to the inset hole and prompt the child just to slide it over into the hole. Make this step as easy as possible if your child has trouble with the fine motor aspect of doing puzzles. You may also introduce foam and rubber puzzles, both inset and interlocking, at this time. Large floor puzzles generally come next, along with small jigsaw puzzles that come in a frame where the jigsaw puzzle is interlocking but set into the frame. These come in both wood and cardboard. If your child seems to enjoy putting puzzles together, I would go ahead and progress to real jigsaw puzzles. I like small jigsaws of about 25 pieces. These are somewhat hard to find, but some sets of wooden puzzles that are packaged four to a box work well. Eventually you can work on 50-100 piece puzzles. By this time, puzzle-making should be a cooperative event, with at least two people working on the puzzle at a time. If a puzzle takes more than a few minutes to complete (more than 25 or so pieces), then it should be taught as a cooperative activity. Puzzling can be a social activity.

Everyone has his or her own method of working jigsaw puzzles. I like to show the child first to lay out all the pieces. Use a large board to put the puzzle on, so if you don't finish it in one sitting you can move it if you need to get it out of the way. Using a board is a good habit for later puzzling of 500-1000 pieces in late (or second) childhood. With these puzzles you should next do the border. Show the child what the border pieces look like, and work on finding them. Then pick something out of the picture that the child can work on—a specific person or thing. Help the child pick out the pieces that might go to that one specific part of the puzzle, and when you find a piece that you might think will fit somewhere, prompt the child to try it there. Children will need a lot of help with big puzzles, and you might have to do larger puzzles in several stages.

I am pretty compulsive about keeping my puzzles organized. I assigned every puzzle that I bought a number. I cut out the picture on the box, and I used a marker to write the assigned number on the back of the picture. I picked up every piece and put the same number on it as well. If it was an inset puzzle, I labeled the base of the inset with an assigned number as well as all the inset pieces. I kept the picture from the box and all the pieces in large zip lock bags. I continued this organization until we progressed to working much larger puzzles. Those puzzles I was able to store in their original boxes.

CONSTRUCTION TOYS

Construction toys are toys that make a definite object (rather than manipulatives, which are more flexible). My son liked the drill toys that have a battery-operated toy drill functioning as a screwdriver or a bolt driver. You can put cars and trucks together with it. The pieces for these toys were large and easy to manipulate, although I generally put the item in place and helped my child to drill the screw or bolt. As you show your child how to do these activities, realize that you might have to help in every step. Keep the picture from the box so your child will know there is a definite object to be produced.

Other construction toys involve snapping together parts to make a figure (for example the Toy Story 2 figurines come in snap-together forms) or those "transforming" figurines that change from one form to another with several steps. For example, with several steps, a figurine T-Rex might transform into a car.

OPEN-END TOYS AND VEHICLES

These toys do not have a definite beginning and end, and play with them may be expanded indefinitely into cooperative building and pretend play. These types of toys are frequently miniature representations of inanimate objects used by adults. One of the most common forms of miniature pretend play is play with vehicles of all types. Play with these toys is not limited to the toy itself. Much car and truck play, in particular, involves more than the play with the vehicle itself; the construction of the track and road can be a prolonged, open-ended activity that leads to more sophisticated play. This construction is a part of the play and should not be skipped over to get to the action and pretend activities. When playing with vehicles, spend plenty of time building a road, track, or city with the child, talking about each aspect of the construction. This building time sets the stage for further development of pretend play with these miniatures.

Many children love to play with toy cars, trucks, construction equipment, and boats. As with any toy or activity, try to find out what your child likes. If he or she likes Thomas the Tank Engine, use that interest to expand his or her play as much as possible, creating tracks and railroads and arranging and talking about the engines and cars. Consider finding a public train table (at the local toy store or bookstore) where your child can be exposed to other children playing with the trains. This informal parallel play experience will be reinforcing to the child since he or he will be playing with a highly favored toy.

If the child receives toys that he or she has no interest in, consider putting them away until a later date. For example, my kid received a large number of miniature cars (Hot Wheels or Matchbox size) as presents, and we played with them and his miniature car city to some extent; but he didn't really show a great interest in miniature toy car play until a few years later. He enjoyed playing with the larger vehicles (Tonka Toy size) as a preschooler. Older children as well as preschoolers frequently play with the smaller vehicles, so keep in mind that if the child has no interest in them at first, when he or she is older, you might reintroduce them. With older children, the toy car play is different from that of younger children and focuses on racing and crashing. Older children may have motorized components to their car play, with supplies that can propel the little cars around a track. Older children may also use battery operated remote control cars. For younger children, I would stick with the simple unmotorized play by building your track or road and moving the vehicles around. Racing concepts may be introduced later.

Types of Vehicles
Many types of vehicles are available for children's play. Preschool vehicles are usually larger and simpler in design than the miniatures designed for older children. Some vehicles designed for preschoolers also include related figurines and accessories (for example, a firetruck will come with figurine firefighters). Vehicle types include:

➢ Rescue vehicles (police cars, fire engines, ambulances)
➢ Tonka Toy size cars and trucks
➢ Doll sized cars
➢ Construction vehicles
➢ Construction crane
➢ Wooden train sets with engines and cars
➢ Boats

- ➢ Airplanes and helicopters
- ➢ School bus with figurines
- ➢ Miniature cars
- ➢ Remote control cars

Supplies

When playing with vehicles, have some supplies available to create a play world for the vehicles. You can create your vehicle world on the floor or carpet using a variety of supplies and props. A road or city mat can help guide you in your layouts. These mats have roads, tracks, and locations (such as the airport) printed on them. You can create your own playmat with poster board, drawing the child's favorite and familiar locations on it. You can use the play mat to help organize your play world, although the mats are not required. Supplies that you might keep on hand for vehicle play include:

- ➢ Road or city mat
- ➢ Play garage
- ➢ Sandbox or yard for larger vehicles
- ➢ Wooden blocks of various sizes
- ➢ Set furnishings (figures, trees, little buildings)
- ➢ Racetracks and racetrack mats
- ➢ Train tracks and accessories
- ➢ Miniature car city parts (tracks, a fire station, McDonalds, service station)
- ➢ Racing ramps and ramp jumps

Components of vehicle play

For specific targets for early vehicle play, see the example imitative play targets in the imitative play section (see page 19). Components of vehicle play include building the set, which might be a road, track, racetrack, or town. The set may be built and furnished with a variety of supplies from the child's toy chest and from around the house. Don't limit yourself to the accessories that go with the particular vehicle. Mix and match your furnishings from any source. You and the child might put assorted figurines around the track, or use blocks to make buildings. Help the child vary props, and use substitutions to stimulate his pretend and imaginative skills. After the set is built and furnished as simply or elaborately as you and the child like, start placing the vehicles in the scene while identifying and talking about them. Vehicle actions can include moving the vehicles around and perhaps racing them or crashing them. The vehicles can go to particular locations. Utility vehicles can perform their duties (for example, a dump truck can be loaded and unloaded). Construction sites are fun to create outside in the yard or in the sandbox.

Note that most vehicles don't have personalities that allow you to talk for them. An exception is the Thomas the Tank Engine characters. Although one can talk for these characters, it is more likely that the child will talk about the character rather than for him. For example, he or she might say, "Here's Bertie the bus" or "Thomas has two coaches" rather than carry on a dialogue between the trains. If your child is a Thomas the Tank Engine fan, he or she might want to act out scenes from the videos or books, so be prepared to jump in and do the theme with him. This preparation requires knowing in detail all the videos or books the child might have seen about the character.

I watched some typical kids play at the train table at the bookstore this weekend. There was a baby, a 3-year-old type, and two boys who looked in the 4-6 year old range. The baby just watched and moved his train a few inches back and forth. The 3-year-old did a lot of "watching" and "imitation" of sounds that the older boys made. The 4-6 year old set did a lot of "Look at me!" type talk and invited the other kids to "Chase my train." Not a single kid made comments on what the others were doing—unless they wanted to join in. For instance, one child had the breakdown train and was hanging a boat from it. Another kid stopped and said "Ah! It is hanging. Here, hang this one" and he briefly joined the first kid trying to convince him to hang another object. The kid with the breakdown train humored this boy for a moment and then went back to his own little world before looking up at me and saying " "Look! Its magic." The narratives were self-narratives. Ironic really since that is exactly what we were trying to get our child to STOP doing a year ago.

Chapter 5
In Vivo Pretend Play

- *Single-Action Pretend*
- *Multiple-Action Pretend*
- *Daily Routines and Familiar Activities*
- *Places to Go*
- *Dress-Up and Character Pretend*
- *Pretend Play Centers and Social Pretend Play*

I divide pretend play into *in vivo* pretend play, *in vitro* pretend play, and pretend play with miniatures. This is an artificial classification, but I find it helpful in describing the different ways a child can pretend. During *in vivo* pretend play, the child is using his or her body to pretend with or without props. The child is personally acting out different activities and scenes or pretending to be various characters and people. In contrast, a child pretending *in vitro* (see Chapter 6) pretends using a representation of an animate object (such as a doll, figurine, puppet, or paper or felt doll). In this case, the child is moving and acting for the figurine rather than being in the play himself or herself. The figurine has its own personality that the child creates. Pretending with miniatures (representations of inanimate objects such as vehicles) represent another form of pretend play that has been discussed in Chapter 4.

In vitro pretend tends to occur at a higher developmental level than *in vivo* pretend and is very sophisticated. I do not believe it should be given much attention until later in the child's program. Instead, I would begin teaching pretending with *in vivo* pretend activities.

Programs that teach advanced pretending require a fair amount of language, so they are easier to teach if the child has some basic conversational skills and can describe events as they occur or retell a situation from the past. However, because pretend play can help develop language skills, simple pretend should probably be introduced sooner, perhaps as soon as the child understands the instructions and prompts. Nonverbal imitation should be strong, however, before you try to teach these skills.

SINGLE-ACTION PRETEND

These early *in vivo* pretend skills teach the child to pretend simple actions. These skills include pretending with props, pretending to use objects that are not present, and pretending to be something or someone that the child is not. These targets require only a few actions or verbalizations and don't require extensive sequencing.

Teaching Procedure

Use an imitative format. Nonverbal imitation should be very strong at this point. Tell the child, "Pretend you are ____" or "Let's pretend we are ____" and model the response for the child. Sometimes children can learn these early targets without any props, but if they require props to understand what is going on, the progression of pretending with props can be as follows:

1. Use the real item (real telephone)
2. Use a pretend item that is a realistic representation of the object (toy telephone)
3. Use a "substitute" item (a wooden block to stand for a phone)
4. Omit props

Keep in mind that we are teaching the child to pretend, not to become a professional mime. Using props is appropriate behavior, and the ability to use substitutions such as that described in Step 3 is an important pretending skill. If the child spontaneously uses substitution props, be sure to reinforce this behavior. It is not necessary to omit props in pretend play.

After introducing a simple pretend action, shape the child's initial responses into greater and more detailed elaboration. Expand on the initial target by adding sound effects and additional actions on an ad-lib basis. Be sure to exaggerate motions and sounds. For example, when pretending to drink from a cup, make gulping noises or slurping noises. Say "Ahhhhh, good tea" when finished. Try to pick actions that are entertaining to the child to help reinforce the behavior as fun. Jot down notes of the elaborations used with the child and of any spontaneous elaborations by the child. The basic action, which should remain fairly consistent, can be decided upon in advance by all the tutors. Animal targets always include the characteristic sound effects of the animal. Other verbalizations can be added as the tutor and child play—"We are pretending to be airplanes—buzzzzzz." If the child verbalizes what he or she is doing or takes the lead, the tutor is free to follow for as long as appropriate pretend can be sustained. It is important to try to make the pretending fun—the sillier the better!

To shape for better motor approximations, you might have to teach some actions individually. It took us some time for us to teach our child how to mold his hand into a cup. He had the concept of pretending to drink, but he would just put his fist to his mouth. Don't get carried away with creating perfect form though. The child is not a mime.

Basic Actions
➢ Drinking from a cup (hot and cold)
➢ Eating with a spoon (hot and cold)
➢ Brushing or combing hair
➢ Licking an ice cream cone
➢ Brushing teeth
➢ Driving a car
➢ Washing face/hands
➢ Stirring food
➢ Banging a drum
➢ Writing
➢ Cutting

- Riding a horse
- Sweeping/vacuuming/mopping/cleaning
- Putting on pants/shirts/socks/shoes/hat/boots/coat
- Surfing
- Playing baseball—batting /throwing/catching
- Talking on the phone
- Pouring from a pitcher
- Holding a baby
- Hitting a nail with a hammer
- Blowing out candles on a birthday cake

Animals
- Dog
- Cat
- Snake
- Chicken
- Cow
- Penguin
- Elephant
- Pig
- Horse
- Flamingo (stand on one leg and tuck your head under an arm)
- Monkey
- Frog
- Bird
- The Very Hungry Caterpillar (crawl around "chomping" on everything in sight making loud chewing sounds)

Things and Fantasy
- Giant
- Train
- Airplane
- Teapot
- Spiders (with your hands—smash each other's spiders!)
- Earthquake—shake around in your chairs

My child liked pretending to do really exciting things, like crashing cars, shooting something, and dropping dead. That's what he liked—drama and excitement.

Simple Charades
This is an excellent activity to reinforce pretend skills. Put the child's known targets on cards—either as a drawing or in words (if your child can read). Teach the child to act out what is on the card without saying what he or she is doing. To play the game, each player draws a card in turn and acts out what is on the card. The other players try to guess what he or she is pretending. The person who guesses right gets a reinforcer and gets to take a turn acting. The actor always gets a reinforcer!

DAILY ROUTINES AND FAMILIAR ACTIVITIES

After the child knows several simple pretend actions, begin to introduce longer sequences of actions. Use activities that the child is familiar with such as "going to school." This sequence may include getting dressed, washing the face, brushing teeth, eating breakfast, putting on a backpack, and waving goodbye. When initially teaching a routine, ask the child to narrate the actions as he or she is pretending them, for example, "I'm eating my cereal," and "I'm brushing my teeth." This narration will help him or her remember the sequence. Later, the narration can be discontinued. Continue to add sequences of behaviors from everyday life. To help develop your child's ability to create pretend sequences, have the child label his or her behaviors as he actually does them in real life. This labeling will make it easier for the child to remember the routines when he or she starts pretending them. The child may use props, but encourage substitutions (using a block to represent soap, for example).

Avoid teaching your child to mime—forcing him or her to render exact physical replications of a routine. Remember that we are teaching pretending, an activity that should be fun for the child. Don't get so carried away with teaching these sequences that you are having your child act out the minutiae of a daily routine. Save the exquisite details for fun pretending like being a Jedi Knight. Extensive detailed physical elaboration of a bath ritual, for example, is not only *not* reinforcing or fun; it is, in fact, sort of weird.

Also remember that you are teaching the child to pretend daily routines and familiar activities. So, you need to expose your child to these activities before he or she can pretend them. Don't try to teach a child to start pretending something he or she is totally unfamiliar with.

Example of Daily Routines and Familiar Activities
➢ Going to school
➢ Going to bed
➢ Eating breakfast
➢ Going shopping
➢ Taking a bath
➢ Doing any sort of baby doll pretend
➢ Baking a cake
➢ Setting a table
➢ Washing/drying/ironing/folding clothes
➢ Making a sandwich
➢ Washing dishes

PLACES TO GO

You can pretend to go to fun and familiar places. Talk about what you will do there and act it out. Books and videos that show these places and the actions associated with them can be helpful resources, especially for places that your child cannot actually go (for example, the jungle). Use helpful books and videos such as the Richard Scarry's *BusyTown* series or the *Spot* series (*Spot goes to the Beach, Spot Goes to the Circus*). When starting to teach about a new place, stick with a just a few props and actions. For example, to go to the beach, put on your swimsuits, get a couple of buckets and shovels and pretend to dig in the sand at the beach (use a brown towel for the sand). As you progress, you can pack your car (two chairs side by side) and drive to the beach. Elaborations can include swimming and jumping in the waves, getting an ice cream cone, flying a kite, looking for seashells, and building a sand castle. If you have a sandbox, move the play there and continue to add actions and conversation. These pretend activities will lead to dress-up and pretend play centers with even more props and actions.

Examples of places to go include:
➤ Beach
➤ Farm
➤ School
➤ Circus
➤ Airport
➤ Ice cream store
➤ Restaurant
➤ Grocery store
➤ McDonald's
➤ Jungle
➤ Ocean
➤ Camping/fishing
➤ Birthday party
➤ The movies
➤ Video store
➤ Car trip

DRESS-UP AND CHARACTER PRETEND

In these activities, the child pretends to be another person. He or she dresses up like a character and does some of the actions and verbalizations associated with the person. The child should know who community helpers are and be familiar with their roles. He or she should also be able to identify characters in movies or in books. Because we are teaching the child to play, I would avoid a lot of academic drilling during this activity, such as asking the child formal questions about the various occupations. We are teaching the child to explore and pretend, not to memorize the details of an occupation. There is always the temptation to sneak in a bunch of drills during play, but I would be careful about that. Many children can sense "work" from a mile away, and you don't want to kill play. Dress-up will naturally lead to play in pretend play centers, and the targets will transfer from dress-up to pretend play center activities as you progress with pretend programs.

Teaching Procedure
Dress-up starts with some basic imitative targets. Get out the costume and the props for a character and show the child how to put them on and use them. Don't worry too much if the child wants to do the same character over and over. Mine that interest, and expand on it. Much of childhood pretend play is repetitive. I think we get so scared of our children's getting stuck on something that we don't let them repeat themes

even as much as normal children do. Repetition can build depth if you continue to expand on what the child is doing. If the child wants repeatedly to dress up as a pirate, for example, keep expanding on his or her pirate repertoire, adding new activities and verbalizations. If he or she likes dressing up as a firefighter, set up a pretend play center and act out entire fire-fighting scenes, adding as much language and as many movements as you can. Be sure to encourage the use of symbolic props; for example, use a jump rope for the fire hose or a chair for a ladder.

Be sure you and your tutors are highly energetic and animated. Ham up all the actions and verbalizations, making the play exciting and reinforcing. Dress up some yourself and join the play. Do not be afraid of active play, sword fights and "killing" each other. Some boys love to sword fight, battle, and chase. Remember that your male child needs to be able to play with peers at some point. You might be squeamish about the violence, but this pretend combat is how many boys play, and some experts feel that this type of boy play helps the children deal with aggression. I don't know whether violent play has that purpose or not, but my kid loved sword play, so I played it with him.

When you are "killed," ham it up, swoon, and fall over. Then see if the child will do the same when you "kill" him or her. Make sure and emphasize that *no* aggressive play occurs unless both parties have a weapon in hand. That is, the child can't come up to you and start hitting you with a sword if you are unarmed or haven't agreed to play. Also, teach the child to hit the swords together rather than hitting the person.

Finally, stick with the basics. You don't need to teach your child to pretend to be a molecular biologist doing DNA sequencing. Stick with familiar community helpers, occupations, and favored fictional characters. My child loved dress-up. He became extremely inventive in using props. He got a lot of ideas from videos and movies and learned to imitate and copy how the people on the screen looked and what they did. A useful idea is to watch a movie about a character or read a book and then immediately go to dress up using props that you have readily available. If the child likes the dress-up character, you can expand on the play with props that you can create.

My child plays dress-up as a paleontologist, Superman, Pajamanaut, astronaut, doctor, or construction worker. He likes to pretend that he is a paleontologist. He makes one of us lie down and be a "fossil." He digs us out with his tools. He also looks for real fossils in our yard. He has a miniature tool kit that he uses. He keeps the fossils he finds in a small plastic container (sort of like a miniature tackle box).

Materials for Dress-Up Costumes

You don't have to buy most of your props aside from some cheap plastic props specific to a character. We have used old suit coats, snow boots, fabric scraps, old hats, belts, and scarves. Keep a couple of boxes of this stuff on hand to use. Before you give away an old item of clothing, think about putting it in the box for future dress-up use. My child had about one-half of his closet filled with dress-up materials at one time. I have made a few items, and I have also bought some costumes that my child specifically requested (*Star Wars* characters), but many of his props were items already in the house. Also keep on hand any sort of uniform or equipment that you use either at work or at play—such as scrubs, hats, sports equipment, and tools. Although I have given long lists of props for each character in the tables below, just start with a few to see if your child is interested in the character. If so, then you can expand your props and activities as you progress.

Items that I specifically made for use in dress-up included vests. These were cut from felt after I drew an easy pattern on a large sheet of paper. You can sew up the two sides or find someone to do it for you. Many dress-up characters use vests, including pirates, cowboys, construction workers, police officers, and train conductors. Dress-up items can be decorated with any sort of craft item glued on, and Velcro will stick to items made from felt as well. If you make up some vests, you can do the decorating on a playdate as part of your arts and crafts project. I also made crowns and hats from felt. These can be closed with iron-on Velcro, and they can provide another craft project for playdates. Cardboard shields can be cut out from any large cardboard box. Attach a handle to the back of the shield and let the child paint it and decorate it. Moneybags (for pirates and knights) can be made of a piece of square cloth. Sew down all the edges to make a hem. Leave two adjacent hems open and thread a piece of cord through the hem to make a purse-string bag.

Dress-up and Character-Pretend Targets

After doing these activities with the child, it is important to write down the basics of what happened. This written record provides a guide for further expansion of the activity the next time you play with the child. It also gives the next person working with the child a definite starting point. This written record can also warn if the child has become stuck in an activity, doing the same thing over and over with no progression or variation. These notes do not have to be extensive; a running list of items under each target is sufficient. New ideas from the tutors should be listed here as well, so they can be tried with the child. These ideas should not form a strict script for the child; rather they should be a list of actions and activities that can be explored. Any spontaneous activities created by the child should be listed as well. These targets are the most exciting and should be strongly reinforced. Note that many of these characters will be used in the pretend play centers, so a written record of actions will provide guidance in playing in those centers as well.

Strictly written scripts for pretend play should be used with caution. Although it might seem an advantage for the child to have "something to say" in a play situation by repeating a memorized script, this technique has several drawbacks. First, it doesn't translate well to playdates: peers won't know the script and won't appreciate having to act out rehearsed dialogue. They want to play, not act. Second, if your child has problems with rigidity, you will have trouble getting him or her to do anything else besides exactly what is written. Third, adults who have no clue about what is appropriate dialogue for pretend play usually write the scripts. Finally, having a child act out a strictly written playscript gives only the appearance of play. While this appearance may perhaps satisfy an adult need to observe the child performing seemingly normal behavior, it does not constitute actual play.

The child can use more loosely written scripts such as those he or she has seen in videos or read in books. These scripts tend to be low on dialogue and high on action. They are more reinforcing to the child and more likely to be known by peers as well. For example, the children might want to act out a scene from a Pokemon video where they pretend to thrown their Pokeballs and have their Pokemons battle each other.

Using scripts from videos and books, however, has some drawbacks as well. My child, for example, liked to act out the generator Jedi fight scene from *The Phantom Menace*. When he first started doing this, we were pleased because he knew the action well and wanted to act out the sequence exactly as it was presented in the movie. This *echo-play-lia* soon turned out to be a disadvantage though, as he would not tolerate deviation from the script, and this rigidity made improvisation (i.e., playing Jedi Knights in general) very difficult.

> *I am leery of play scripts. My consultant handed me a sheet of them once at a workshop. I never used them. I didn't use them because if you say to my child, "You are a pirate and I am a lost boy," he can role-play fights, being captured, etc. He doesn't need to read from a script. The other concern I had was that if you tell him to read a "script," he is prone to getting upset if you deviate from the script (although he isn't picky about himself sticking to the script). When I tried to deviate from the written script once, he stopped the play and said, "No. You're supposed to say ____!"*

Dress-up and Character-Pretend Examples

➢ Doctor
➢ Construction worker
➢ Police officer
➢ Firefighter
➢ Pirate
➢ King or queen
➢ Superman
➢ Spiderman
➢ Batman
➢ Train conductor
➢ Star Wars characters and other fictional characters from books and videos
➢ Cowboy
➢ Race car driver
➢ Farmer
➢ Hairdresser
➢ Photographer (animal safari)
➢ Bus driver
➢ Hairdresser

Pretending Dress-up and Character Examples

Under each character I list some possible props and some early pretending ideas. For early play, you will give the child a few specific things to do and say. These early play ideas will introduce the character to the child and some of the actions associated with the character. Later, you will create short sequences with the child, working towards more interactive play between the child and the tutor. These stories should be simple and straightforward with an emphasis on action. I demonstrate how this is done with the firefighter example. When pretending any story sequence with the child, the tutor must be very energetic, animated, and a major ham!

FIREFIGHTER

Prop Ideas

➢ Fire coat (use an old black pea coat or raincoat)
➢ Boots (snow boots)
➢ Fire hat, belt, badge, fire ax, and radio (plastic toy set)
➢ Fire truck (two chairs)
➢ Stuffed Dalmatian dog
➢ Fire hose (jump rope, Toobers and Zots, outside garden hose)
➢ Firefighter books and videos (*Sesame Street Firehouse*, *Fire trucks for Kids*)

Early Play Ideas

➢ Get dressed (talk about the props and what they are for)
➢ Talk about what firefighters do
➢ Ride in the fire truck (driving and making siren noises)
➢ Sing and act out the Firefighter song (Hurry, hurry, drive the fire truck...)
➢ Spray the water (pretend to be whipped around by the fire hose force)
➢ Talk on the radio
➢ Climb the ladder (chairs or step stools)
➢ Rescue dolls and stuffed animals from building (put on high shelves)

Later Play Ideas

➢ Set up a fire station with a phone.
➢ Set up a fire truck
➢ Set up the burning house
➢ Tutor discovers fire—smoke alarms, smelling smoke, seeing the fire
➢ Tutor "calls" firefighter and reports fire
➢ Child gets dressed and gets in the fire truck in a hurry!
➢ Drive to the fire (drive through the house with lots of noise and sound effects)
➢ Spray water on the fire
➢ Rescue people (including the tutor, dolls, and stuffed animals)
➢ Go back to the fire station
➢ Get undressed
➢ Take a rest

CONSTRUCTION WORKER/CARPENTER

Prop Ideas

➢ Children's tool kit or small tackle box with real and plastic tools
➢ Tool belt or carpenter's apron
➢ Hard hat
➢ Blocks
➢ Wood boards or unused shelves or a large piece of cardboard

> ➢ Cardboard boxes
> ➢ Pages and pencils for making "blueprints"
> ➢ Children's toy workbench
> ➢ Mailing tape
> ➢ Packing knife (for adult use only)
> ➢ Construction videos and books (*Kid's Construction* videos, *Machines at Work*)
> ➢ Pre-fabricated wood construction kits (The Home Depot makes several)

Pretending Ideas
> ➢ Put on and load the belt or apron with tools
> ➢ Put on the hard hat
> ➢ Build a "house" (put shelves on the seats of two chairs facing each other and pretend to hammer the roof on
> ➢ Build a house with cardboard boxes (tutor can do the cutting and taping)
> ➢ Build a doghouse for the stuffed animals (use cardboard boxes and tape)
> ➢ Drive the dump truck (use the bed as the dump truck and put a board or piece of cardboard on the bed. Pile blocks on the board, drive the truck, and then dump the load by lifting up the end of the board and letting the blocks fall on the floor)
> ➢ Drive the bulldozer (have the child walk on his or her knees with a large piece of cardboard in front of him moving blocks around the room; add sound effects)
> ➢ Front loader (use the cardboard to lift up blocks onto the dump truck)
> ➢ Pack a lunch box and eat lunch
> ➢ Use the imitative play targets for the toy workbench
> ➢ Build with the prefabricated construction kits

Vocalization ideas
> ➢ "We're building a house"
> ➢ "Time for lunch"
> ➢ "Hand me my tool box"
> ➢ "I need a hammer"

PIRATE

Prop Ideas
> ➢ Pirate dress-up clothes (vest, eye patch, belt, swords, pistols, bandanas, boots, capes, coats. telescope, money bag with coins, pirate hats, cut-off pants)
> ➢ Outdoor play equipment or table to use as a pirate ship
> ➢ Treasure chest or box with treasures in it
> ➢ Treasure map
> ➢ Hook for hand
> ➢ Crutch for Long John Silver
> ➢ Pirate flag
> ➢ Stuffed parrot

➤ Cardboard box for crow's nest
➤ Pirate books and videos (*Fisher-Price Pirate Ship Book*, *Muppet Treasure Island*)

Pretending Ideas

➤ Dress up and talk about the props. There are different pirate dress-up styles, so vary the dress-up costume.
➤ Have a sword fight
➤ Walk the plank
➤ Look for treasure
➤ Bury the treasure and dig it up
➤ Sing pirate songs from *Muppet Treasure Island* (lyrics are on the World Wide Web)
➤ Walk around using crutch on one leg
➤ Go on a treasure hunt (described in Chapter 7)

Vocalization Ideas

➤ "Arghh matey"
➤ "Now you have to walk the plank"
➤ "We're sailing for adventure"
➤ "Let's find the treasure"
➤ "Polly want a cracker?"

KNIGHT

Prop Ideas

➤ Man's suit coat
➤ Wide belt or sash
➤ Bow and arrow set (I found a soft foam set that is easy to use)
➤ Sword
➤ Commercial knight dress-up costume
➤ Shield (make from cardboard or purchase)
➤ Old-fashioned hobby horse
➤ Hat or helmet
➤ Boots
➤ Money bag

Pretending Ideas

➤ Watch *Dragonheart, Robin Hood* and other knight-related videos
➤ Have a sword fight with shields
➤ Shoot bows and arrows
➤ Target practice with bows and arrows
➤ Ride a horse
➤ Talk to the King (teach the child how to kneel and put a sword in front of his or her body)
➤ Slay the dragon

➢ Rescue the Damsel in Distress (a princess trapped in a tower—use the closet)
➢ Wake the sleeping princess (with a kiss)
➢ Knight the Knight (have the king touch the sword to the knight's shoulders)

Vocalization Ideas

➢ "I'm here to serve you, your majesty."
➢ "The king commands it."
➢ "The peasants are revolting!"
➢ "I am a knight of the old code."
➢ "I will defend the weak!"
➢ "You're my knight in shining armor!"

COWBOY/WESTERN SHERIFF

Prop Ideas

➢ Cowboy prop set
➢ Vest
➢ Cowboy boots
➢ Hobby horse
➢ Guns and holster
➢ Rope
➢ Stuffed animals
➢ Branding iron
➢ Blocks
➢ Sheriff's badge
➢ Bandanas
➢ Cowboy hats and boots
➢ Money bags for the "bad guy" to steal

Pretending Ideas

➢ Ranching (corral the herd of stuffed animals and drive the cattle)
➢ Rope a horse or cow (the tutor can be the cow!)
➢ Brand a cow
➢ Ride a horse
➢ Ride a bucking bronco
➢ Ride a horse using tutor as horse
➢ Stampede! (let a herd of stuffed animals fall down the stairs)
➢ Cook food and eat around the campfire (made with blocks)
➢ Have a gunfight
➢ Stage a train robbery or stagecoach robbery
➢ Arrest the "bad guy"
➢ Put the "bad guy" in jail

Vocalization Ideas
➤ "Let's round up these doggies."
➤ "Yee haw!"
➤ "Stampede!"
➤ "I'm the law around here!"
➤ "Stick 'em up!"
➤ Campfire songs

PHOTOGRAPHER/ANIMAL SAFARI

Prop Ideas
➤ Polaroid camera with film
➤ Stuffed animals
➤ Small photo album to put the pictures in

Pretending Ideas
➤ Go on photographic adventures such as a nature walk or photographic safari (put stuffed animals out all over the yard, let the children find the animals, and photograph them)
➤ Have the children take portrait photos of each other in regular and dress-up clothes

Vocalization Ideas
➤ "Smile for the camera."
➤ "Say cheese."
➤ "Look, there's a tiger!"
➤ "I took a picture!"
➤ "Smile for the camera."
➤ "Look at the pictures from my safari!"

PRETEND PLAY CENTERS AND SOCIAL PRETEND PLAY

A pretend play center provides a setting where children can learn social pretend play. These centers are commonly found in preschool and kindergarten classrooms. The interactive pretend play created by children in these centers helps them to understand relationships and interactions among people. Children learn by practicing with their peers the adult behaviors and language that they have observed. This practice helps them build self-confidence with new situations and concepts. By pretending with peers in a structured pretend play center, children can learn to plan, sequence, negotiate, and problem-solve with each other. They can learn the concepts of turn-taking, sharing, and fairness. Participation in pretend play centers therefore represents an important goal for our children. However, our children will need to be taught in a formal manner to participate in pretend play centers. Practice in a non-threatening setting with an adult in a one-on-one manner will ultimately give the child the confidence to interact with peers. Peers can be faded in as the child progresses.

Structure of Pretend Play Centers

These centers develop from the dress-up types of activities. Pretend play centers are more involved than dress-up in that they have a structured space in which the children pretend, and usually more than one role is involved. The defined space provided by these centers allows two or more children to organize their play. The structure gives the children a known reference, and it makes it easier for peers to play with your child. Finally, the structure itself gives the children a storyline to follow—certain events generally happen in a store, for example—and the children can act out the different roles.

To teach in a pretend play center, first decide what sort of center you want to create. Have the child help you gather the props and build the center with the child. Discuss the center and props with the child while you are building. Label the items as you put them into the center and provide plenty of commentary. Ask lots of questions and prompt answers. Have the child practice the different roles and switch them frequently. Make some mistakes yourself, like putting the food on the floor, if you are playing the waiter, and prompt the child to correct you.

PRETEND PLAY CENTER IDEAS

STORES

Props
- Large cardboard boxes for counters and shelves
- Paper bags or plastic grocery bags for purchases
- Toy cash register
- Play money
- Toy telephone
- Shopping cart or basket
- Chalkboard/white board for signs or paper and tape for posters
- Post-it note pad for "receipts" and markers
- Telephone
- Grocery store—empty cereal boxes, clean juice and milk cartons, plastic food
- Toy Store—toys
- Bookstore—books
- Video rental store—videos
- Pet store—small pets and stuffed animals

Roles
Shopper
- Pushes a cart or carries a basket
- Selects items and takes them to cashier
- Waits for the cashier to ring them up
- Pays the cashier

Sample vocalizations:
"Good morning."
"I would like to buy these things."
"Here's my money."
"Thank you."

Cashier
  ➢ Waits at the counter
  ➢ Rings up the shopper's purchase and uses the cash register
  ➢ Gives a receipt and change
  ➢ Packs the purchases into bags for shopper

Sample vocalizations:
"Good morning."
"That will be $____."
"Here's your change."
"Thank you for shopping here!"

Salesperson
  ➢ Puts items on the shelves and writes on the chalkboard
  ➢ Asks if the shopper needs help
  ➢ Helps shopper

BAKERY

The bakery is similar to the store center except that you should locate the bakery in the kitchen and help the kids bake. Then put the goodies out for the children to "sell" to each other.

DOCTOR'S OFFICE/VETERINARY OFFICE

Props
  ➢ Child's medical kit (supplemented with household medical supplies)
  ➢ Bandages
  ➢ Dolls and stuffed animals
  ➢ Tongue depressor
  ➢ Ace bandage
  ➢ Braces, crutches, or other medical supplies from around the house
  ➢ Doctor's costume kit or white coat
  ➢ Scales
  ➢ Table for the patient to sit and lie on
  ➢ Clipboard with paper and pen for the "chart"
  ➢ Post-it note pad for "prescriptions"
  ➢ Empty pill and elixir bottles

Roles
Doctor

➤ Greets patient
➤ Weighs and measures patient
➤ Looks in the ears
➤ Shines a light in eyes
➤ Looks in the mouth
➤ Listens to chest
➤ Feels the patient's tummy
➤ Gives a "shot"
➤ Puts on a brace or bandage
➤ Writes in the "chart"
➤ Gives a post-it note as prescription
➤ Gives the patient a pill or elixir bottle (empty)

Sample vocalizations:
"Hello, I'm your doctor. My name is Dr. _____."
"Let's see how much you weigh."
"I'm going to look into your ears."
"I have to give you a shot."
"Be sure to eat your vegetables."
"You are doing fine. See you next time!"
"Say 'ahh.'"
"Take this medicine so you can get better."

Patient

➤ Follows the instructions from doctor
➤ Tells the doctor his or her problem

Sample Vocalizations:
"Doctor, I hurt my leg."
"Ahh!"
"Oh no, I don't want a shot!"
"That didn't hurt too much."
"Ok, doctor, I'll take my medicine."

Pet owner

➤ Gives stuffed animal pet to vet to examine
➤ Tells the vet what the problem is
➤ Holds the stuffed animal while the vet examines it
➤ Comforts the stuffed animal pet

SCHOOL

In this pretend center, your child can practice school and circle time activities in a less serious manner than in an actual school situation. Here in the school center, the child can pretend to be the teacher or the student. I make a distinction between pretending to do a circle time (play) and actually doing a circle time (work!).

Props
➢ Table/chairs
➢ Books/coloring books
➢ Pencils/crayons
➢ White board or chalkboard with chalk or dry-erase pens
➢ Eraser
➢ Pointer
➢ Stuffed animals and dolls to be extra students
➢ Place for circle time
➢ "Good job" stickers and stars

Roles
Teacher
➢ Stands at the whiteboard/chalkboard with pointer
➢ Writes on the blackboard/chalkboard
➢ Calls on students
➢ Gives "time outs" to disruptive students
➢ Arranges students into a circle or asssigns desks
➢ Lines up students for going out of the classroom
➢ Helps students have a snack/lunch
➢ Runs circle time that may include story time, songs, counting, and show-and-tell.

Sample vocalizations:
"Good morning, class."
"It's circle time—everyone come sit down."
"Arthur, come write your name on the board."
"Now we are going to sing."
"Let's count."
"Mary, you are not listening. You need a time-out."

Student
➢ Sits at a desk
➢ Sits in circle time and participates
➢ Answers questions from the teacher
➢ Writes on paper
➢ The tutor as student can be disruptive and prompt the child to correct him or her!

KITCHEN CENTER

The kitchen center is the classic kindergarten pretend play center. If you have a play kitchen, use the imitative steps in Chapter 2 to start teaching play in this center. Expand the play to include having tea parties, cooking, serving, and eating meals, putting away groceries from the grocery store, and cooking and serving food.

RESTAURANT

Props
- ➢ Table and chairs
- ➢ Candle sticks and candleholders, flowers, or other centerpieces
- ➢ Order pad for the waiter
- ➢ Apron or towel (to drape over the arm) for the waiter
- ➢ Tray for the waiter to carry
- ➢ Menus
- ➢ Tablecloth, place mats, and napkins
- ➢ Play food or blocks to represent food
- ➢ Telephone
- ➢ Cash register and play money

Roles
Diners
- ➢ Dress up in "fancy" dress-up clothes
- ➢ Wait to be seated and sit at the table
- ➢ Look at the menus
- ➢ Talk to the waiter—order food
- ➢ Eat and drink
- ➢ Pay the waiter

Chef
- ➢ Wears chef's hat and apron
- ➢ Comes to talk to diners
- ➢ Prepares play or real food

Waiter
- ➢ Uses apron, towel, pencil and pad
- ➢ Seats diners
- ➢ Gives out menus
- ➢ Takes orders
- ➢ Brings food on a tray
- ➢ Takes money

CAMPING

Pretending to go camping is fun for children. If the weather is nice set up your pretend play center outside and pretend to do all the activities you would do on a campout.

Props

- ➢ Any camping supplies you have—tents, sleeping bags, canteens, etc.
- ➢ Children's play tent
- ➢ Children's indoor sleeping bag, blankets, and pillows
- ➢ Backpacks and fanny packs
- ➢ Children "adventure" play set (plastic set with binoculars, knife, canteen, etc.)
- ➢ Wooden blocks
- ➢ Sticks or skewers for roasting marshmallows
- ➢ Marshmallows
- ➢ Pretend fishing lines or sticks with string
- ➢ Lantern
- ➢ Flashlights
- ➢ Stuffed animals
- ➢ Camping books and videos (*Just Me and My Dad, Barney's Campfire*)

Activities

- ➢ Build a fire with the blocks and "roast" marshmallows
- ➢ Go fishing—sit on bed and drop lines off the side
- ➢ Cook fish
- ➢ Turn off the lights and pretend to sit by the fire
- ➢ Use the flashlight
- ➢ Get in the sleeping bag and tent
- ➢ Sing campfire songs
- ➢ Run from the bear
- ➢ Feed the rabbits
- ➢ Make your own tent by draping sheets over a table

LIBRARY

A library pretend center can help the children practice library skills. They can "read" to each other in a pretend storytime.

Props

- ➢ Children's books
- ➢ Date Stamp and Stamp Pad
- ➢ Post-it Notes (can put in back of book and have the "librarian" date-stamp it)

Roles

Librarian

> ➤ Says "shhh."
> ➤ Stamps books
> ➤ Reads stories for storytime

Readers

> ➤ Pick out books
> ➤ Take books to the librarian to stamp

LEMONADE STAND

I would do this pretend play center for real. Make up the lemonade with your child's help. Have the kids make a sign and set out a table for the pitcher, some cups, a money can, and ice. If you don't have a lot of sympathetic traffic, call the neighbors and ask them to come over and "buy" some lemonade (you can subsidize this). Have the children pour the lemonade for the customers and put the money in the can.

Examples of Tutor Notes from Early *in-vivo* Pretend Activities

Note that some of these activities went better than others. We had our worst episodes when the tutors tried to follow a script I wrote. These notes are from some of our early pretend programs after we had finished single-action pretend. Most of our child's later pretend play involving dress-up and pretend play centers was done outside of therapy and in playdates and was not documented.

Camping. First we built a tent with a sheet over the table and chairs. Next, we built a fire with wooden blocks. Eric started the fire by rubbing sticks together. We cooked hot dogs and ate dinner. It got dark, and we went inside the tent using the sword as a flashlight. Eric said, "Now it's time to sleep" but we heard a hoot owl outside. Then he whispered "Uh-oh, I heard a bear." Hannah (the other tutor) snuck up on the tent and attacked us! So cute!

Police Officer. (Here the tutor was trying to follow a written script that involved a police officer finding a lost purse). Eric did not want to be a police officer. He said he couldn't find my purse. He wanted to wear the police vest. He didn't want to put on the police helmet. With a verbal prompt he gave me my purse and said, "Here's your purse."

Superman. (This was another attempt at a prewritten "script") He did not want to put on the cape (which was a sweater). He said, "It's a sweater." I crawled under the table and said, "Help Superman, I'm stuck under here." He reached his hand under the table and pulled me out. Then he shouted that he couldn't be Superman because he was a boy.

Daddy. He put on the pin stripe jacket, the red clip-on tie, and the ball cap. I said, "See you later, Dr. Eric," and he said, "No, I'm Daddy. I got to go to the office now. I'll see you later." Then he went to the study and chattered as if he were talking to someone and then came back and started taking off the coat and tie. He said, "I'm going to be a boy now."

Daddy. He said, "Can we play at the golf course?" He used his tackle box as a golf bag, balloons as golf balls, and a stick horse as a club. Eric's language included "Oh, Julie, come inside the house [the closet]— it's raining." "Will you lock the door with this?" (the stick horse). "It's stopped raining now. Let's go back to the golf course."

Mechanic. Eric dressed up with an army jacket, hard hat, and tool belt. I used a chair as a car and pretended to get a flat. I called for help on a car phone. Language from Eric: "Do you have a flat tire?" "Wait, you need a car." "Hello, I'll be right there." "I'm here to help you." I prompted him to use the other chair as a tow truck.

Grocery Store. We used different colored blocks as food (all Eric's idea). For example, green triangle blocks were lettuce, green rectangle blocks were broccoli, yellow square blocks were fresh corn, yellow rectangle blocks were lemons, red/pink balloons were peaches, and yellow balloons were bananas; and there were several others as well. He identified all the objects and said, "I'm ready to check out." He followed the conversation. I said, "Hello, Sir," and Eric said, "Hello, grocery store lady." HA!

Camping. The bed was a mountain, the closet was a cave, and the chairs were hills. Eric offered, "Let's build a fire and cook hot dogs and pizza," "Oh no! There's a bear in here!" "Are you tired?" "Let's go fishing."

Mailman. Eric wanted to be a mailman. He got paper, folded it, put it in envelope, wrote Mom's name on the front and drew a stamp (he even added the sign for cents). He wanted to deliver the mail to mom. He initiated the entire scenario on his own.

Baking. When we finished playing Hi-Ho Cherry-Os, Eric said he wanted to bake a cherry pie. I said, "Ok, let's do it." He went to his bed and got the little star pillow and started putting cherries on top. When we finished, I asked him what to do next and he said to cook them. We put them in the "oven" (drawer), and he said, "Now we have to wait." After we waited, we took out the pie and ate it.

Snowman. After doing sequencing (drills) with the snowman cards, we decided to build a snowman. He said, "It is January—time to build a snowman." We rolled white pillows into three balls of snow and used Laura's sweater as a scarf. He found blocks for eyes and buttons and put a hat on the top. He used a pen for a carrot nose. We decided to call him Frosty. He said, "The sun is out." I said, "Uh oh, Frosty's melting." He destroyed Frosty, put the stuff back, and said, "Frosty melted!"

Doctor. I had bruises and scrapes on my arms and asked him to fix me up. We got out the doctor kit and Band-Aids and played as if he were bandaging my arms. He was very cooperative throughout. He needed minimal prompting to talk appropriately.

Tea party. (Scripted) He got out cups, plates, napkins, and tea pitcher. He put water in the pitcher. He said it was "great tea" and "I want more please." Used candy for food. Asked for more cookies. He said, "I made them myself." He looked at me and said, "We went on a picnic."

Vet. We were playing with the Arthur and D.W. dolls. They had a car wreck. Eric said, "Oh no, they need a vet." He got out the doctor gear and patched them up. One doll got a shot.

Chapter 6
In Vitro Pretend Play

- *Types of Figurines*
- *Playsets*
- *Individual Characters*
- *Progression of Figurine Play*
- *Figurine Scenes*
- *Figurine Action Pretend with Narration*
- *Talking for Figurines*
- *Social Figurine Play*

In vitro pretend play is pretend play with figurines. It is an advanced skill. In developmental classifications, imaginative figurine play appears towards the end of play development. As I have noted before, many children do not progress far with figurine play. They might carry around a favorite stuffed animal as a young child, carry around and talk about little movie character figurines, or have the figurines act out little scenes with the child as a solitary player. But they may never progress to interactive, multi-player, dialogue-driven social figurine play.

We did not do a lot of formal *in vitro* play activities with my child. By the time we got around to concentrating on them, his peers had moved on to other activities, and I felt his time could be used more effectively in other areas. Although many children play figurines as a solitary activity (for example, the child Andy in *Toy Story*), reciprocal play with figurines (where two children are talking for figures that are talking to each other) is rarer. As we had no peers who played in this manner, we did not stress it.

Unfortunately, when I reviewed some other play programs, I found that most of the activities taught as *in vitro* play were not technically playskill activities. Rather, programs were using these *props* of play to teach social behavior, language, and role-playing. This use of figurines might be a good way to teach social skills, but it is *not* play. Play is non-literal, non-goal-oriented, and self-reinforcing.

In our case, I felt it would be better to teach my child social skills and behavior in other formats. He was almost seven, and I did not want to spend time teaching him to hold, manipulate, and talk for figurines. He did like to carry around his figurines and talk about them. He did this quite a bit with his *Star Wars* figures, but, interestingly, he did not start using dialogue until he watched *Toy Story 2* and got some of those figurines. Now he walks around with those movie figures, arranging them and talking about them, and occasionally having them speak some dialogue. He carries his "Cowboy Woody" doll with him everywhere. This is a solitary activity, though, except for a few brief dialogue exchanges with his older brother.

Observing my older typical son at play, I noticed that he also usually did figurine play alone. He would carry on a running dialogue of the characters he was manipulating, but he would not hold the figurines "correctly"; he would simply say the dialogue he was making up (along with a lot of extra sound effects he liked to add) while moving them into various poses and positions. When playing with another child (a rarer activity), he and the peer would talk mostly about what their figures were doing ("Ok, now let's pretend that she is the princess and she's falling out the window") and do some reciprocal dialogue, but it was very loose and fluid. I rarely saw instances where the children would hold the dolls "correctly" and have them face each other and talk in a strict dialogue. The children shifted focus, scenery, and actions constantly and instantaneously as each child thought of innovations. This play occurred with a tremendous amount of nonverbal communication in which each child just knew what the other meant and was able to shift focus flexibly. There was no written script (no child said to the other, "No, that's not right. She's supposed to fall here").

> *Not a single kid in my playgroup this summer played with figurines—at least they didn't do it with the other kids. They would do some on their own but it was kept parallel. One kid decided to take silly putty and splat Western Town with it while declaring that Western Town was stuck in gum.*

TYPES OF FIGURINES

I use the terms *figurine*, *figure*, *doll*, and *action figure* interchangeably. They all represent animate objects (people, animals, and fantasy figures). They can be little plastic figures, stuffed animals, dolls, 2-D felt figures, Colorforms, paper dolls, or Magi-cloth theater figures. In figurine play, the figurine has a "personality"; that is, the child manipulates the figurine as if it had its own personality and could control its own actions although the child is physically the one moving the object.

By this definition, playing with a baby doll is generally not figurine play. When children play with baby dolls, they are in the play, playing Mommy or Daddy. The doll might cry (the child making the crying sounds), but for the most part, the action is that of the child taking care of the doll—feeding, changing, putting it in bed, and so forth. Similarly, a child might hug a stuffed animal or put it in an adjacent chair at mealtime. In contrast, during figurine play, the child's personality is not in the play; the child projects a personality onto the figure and becomes the physical agent for the words and actions of the figure.

PLAY SETS

Play sets are pre-made sets that usually come with a few figures and props and a setting to play in. Playsets are easy to play with because the setting is fixed and some obvious things to do with the figures are built into the play set. A lot of playtime with these sets is spent in arranging the play set and the figures. Less time is spent in actually creating a specific event and in dialogue. This set-up time is fine: setting up a scene is a definite part of the play, and moving the scenery and figures continues throughout the play. Spend plenty of time teaching the child to set up the playset and move the figures around before trying to invent little scenes with the child.

Playsets (particularly the Fisher Price ones) have developed a negative image for some parents in the Applied Behavioral Analysis (ABA) community. Some parents hate these sets because they were required to teach playing with these sets at the beginning of their play programs. Their children were not ready for figurine play and had no interest in the sets whatsoever. Much pointless time was spent trying to teach the children to manipulate the figures and act out adult-written play scripts (some evidence of this experience can be still be seen in our imitative play drill targets. In retrospect, I think these toys can be useful and enjoyable for the child if he or she is ready for figurines and shows an interest in the subject of the playset. However, I do not think that these playsets are appropriate to introduce in a beginning play program.

Over a year ago, we bought the Little People House, Farm and Airplane playsets, hoping for him to take to playing with figurines. Not a chance. He is just not into this type of play. I finally gave up and took all the Little People stuff to a used clothing/toy store last week. He likes the Rescue Heroes figures, however. He actually pretends stuff with them. Mostly the same thing over and over, but that is what our typical neighbor child does with them as well.

PLAYSET EXAMPLES

Arthur playset—This playset consisted of a long board folded into sections. It could be stood up on its side. Along the sides were buildings in Arthur's life (library, house, school). It came with props like desks, pets, computer, and TV. It even had doors cut into the board so that the figures could go from outside to inside.

Winnie the Pooh—Several Disney characters have playsets. We used the Winnie the Pooh Western Playset.

Large thematic playsets—These large playsets involve a setting such as a castle, boat, or town with figurines and props. Examples include the Fisher Price playsets (Pirate Ship, Western Town, Submarine, and Castle.)

School House playset with playground—This small set was chosen by our child at a yard sale, and he enjoyed playing with it.

Doll houses with furniture and people—Doll houses come in a wide variety of styles, sizes, and materials. We used a large wooden one. We eventually sent this dollhouse to kindergarten with my child to share with the other children. Another popular dollhouse with my child was Maisy's foldout dollhouse. This paper doll house folds into a book when not in use and opens out into a multi-room house. My child enjoyed moving Maisy from room to room and having her use various household items.

Fisher price school bus with figurines

Duplo playsets with figures

Farm and horse playsets

Dinosaur playsets

INDIVIDUAL CHARACTERS

In choosing individual figurines for your child, let commercialism be your guide. Don't impose some unknown figurine on your child just because it is noncommercial and politically correct. Pick figures your child is familiar with. He or she might not have the capacity to invent a personality for an anonymous figure, so give your child one with a built-in personality that he or she already likes.

If the child shows an interest in a character from a book, movie, or TV show, then by all means obtain one. I still see kids carrying around their stuffed Barneys. These figures are generally widely available both at toy stores and at fast-food places. Recent movie characters are good because not only is your child familiar with them, but his or her peers will be playing with them too.

McDonald's and Burger King have the toys that kids play with. We got tons and tons of use out of those dinosaur puppets. Of course, we also had constant requests for the Pokemon from Burger King. The beast machine monsters that are currently at McDonald's are great. They are machines and monsters (wow). The kids who came for playdates were more into the fast-food toys than anything else. Have the tutors or parents make some trips to Burger King and McDonald's for the toys or buy some off Ebay. This sounds trendy and oh so consumerish but these toys are what kids are into. Forget trips to the Dollar Store. Grab a gluten free hamburger bun and run to McDonald's for a happy meal. You can also get in 15 minutes of peer play in the ball pit. If your child isn't playing nicely, you can leave without calling a peer's mom or worrying about what the typical peer thinks since you most likely won't see those typical kids in the ball pit again.

3-D Figures
These stand-alone figures can be used in a variety of settings. Examples include:

➢ Stuffed animals and dolls
➢ Puppets
➢ Animal figurines
➢ Action figures and toy soldiers
➢ GI Joe size male action dolls
➢ Barbie size female figures
➢ Small plastic commercial movie character figurines
➢ Cowboy and Indian sets
➢ Farm and horse sets
➢ Mr. Potato Heads
➢ Transforming figures

2-D Figures
These two-dimensional figures are usually made of felt or paper. Play with these figures tends to be centered on arranging them on a layout and talking about them. Commercial felt products are available, but they are expensive. You can make your own large felt boards with large pieces of presentation board and felt.

2-D figurines include:

➢ Felt people and animals
➢ Colorforms
➢ MagiCloth Theatres figures

PROGRESSION OF FIGURINE PLAY

Figurine play has a developmental progression. The progression described below is not meant to be a strict hierarchy, but rather to serve as a guide to teaching figurine play with your child.

Figurine Scenes
In early figurine play, a child might just carry around the figurines or label them. You can prompt some progression of this activity by setting up scenes and posing the figures in them. Initially, involve the child as well as the figures in the play, creating a combination of *in vivo* and *in vitro* play. For example, include stuffed animals and figurines in your Pretend play centers by having the figures act as students in the School Center or as diners in the Restaurant. The classic example of this mixed *in vivo* and *in vitro* play is the Tea Party with stuffed animals and dolls. Have your child include his or her figurines in a tea party, arranging them around a table, and talking to them and serving them.

> **[Tutor note]** *We built a city with wood blocks, and got people of all sorts out of the toy drawer. We designated a parking garage and put cars in there. We made a jungle separate from the city for Tarzan and Jane because "Tarzan doesn't go in the city." We made a pretend call to the plumber. Eric pretended to make the call and then transferred the play to the figures who finished out the job.*

Introduce playsets next. Have the child help you set up the playset and arrange the figures. You and the child can talk about the figures and the setting. Prompt language about what you are doing ("Where should we put the cow?"). You can arrange a dollhouse and put the dolls in various poses. Or you can set up the props from a small playset. This activity enables the child to become accustomed to handling the figures and setting up little scenes. We originally introduced playsets and figurines in our earliest imitative play drills. My tutor notes from this section reflect that my child had significant difficulty with playsets and figurines. I believe they were too introduced early in his play program. Later, he was able to play with them more effectively.

> **[Tutor note]** *We played sheriff and bad guy with the Fisher Price Western Town. We chased each other on horses. He needed a lot of prompting to respond to statements or questions, but he made his character move appropriately. For example, when I locked him in jail for stealing money—he escaped. When we had a duel, he knocked my guy in the head with his cactus.*

Figurine Action Pretend with Narration
In this form of figurine play, the child holds a figurine (an animal or a person) and moves it through a series of actions. You can prompt this type of play by moving your own figurine and having the child imitate you. You can progress to talking about the actions and encouraging your child to do the same.

For example, you can hold an Obi Wan Kenobi and your child can hold a Han Solo. You say, "Obi Wan is jumping!" and make your figurine jump. Prompt your child to do the same thing with his or her figure ("Make Han jump too!"). Prompt the child to say, "Han is jumping."

Once you can get the child to imitate you with the figure through a variety of chained actions, add in figurine narration. Try to progress to having the child move the figurine into novel actions and describe what is happening: "Rex is knocking down all the blocks!" "He's falling in the water!"

Stick with figures and animals your child likes and is familiar with. You can then encourage your child to start acting out familiar scenes from movies and books using the figures. This development is similar to the *in vivo* progression where the child acts out familiar routines and then progresses to fantasy *in vivo* play.

These figurine action sequences are of known familiar scenes and are different in nature from acting out a play script written by an adult. Acting out an adult-written play script (for example, having the child act out an adult written social story using dolls) is an activity I consider *puppeteering* and *not* play. In puppeteering, a person moves a figure, doll, or puppet according to a preconceived play script with specifically defined actions and dialogue. This activity is not an early play activity (although older children might enjoy putting on scripted puppet shows). In true spontaneous play, the action and words are thought up and done as you go along.

Although acting out short action scenes from books or videos is a minor form of puppeteering as opposed to spontaneous imaginative play, the scripts are usually known action scenes that are reinforcing to the child. They don't usually require a lot of dialogue or lengthy explications. They are more flexible in that the child can vary the actions and dialogue as he or she desires. If the child chooses to act out a part of a video with figurines (example, the peach rolling over the car in *James and the Giant Peach)*, it is a script-driven activity, yes, but the child has chosen it, is reinforced by it, and has had to create the props to carry out the action. While not totally spontaneous, this action involves creativity and pretend skills at work.

Talking for Figurines
In this more advanced form of figurine play, the child begins to use dialogue for the figures. The child is basically talking to himself or herself. The child mixes his or her statements between narration ("Oh, no, he's falling") and figurine talk ("Help me, I'm falling.") Although the figures might talk to each other, the child plays out all the roles. He or she completely controls the play and does not have to adjust to another child's play. This is an advanced and common form of figurine play for children.

> **[Tutor note]** *He played with Arthur and D.W. Carried on appropriate conversation. He wanted them to play with Legos (the "script" called for D.W. to ask Arthur to play beanbags). He had D.W. take out the Legos, play with them, and put them away. He sent D.W. to her room for dumping out the Legos after they were finished.*

Social Figurine Play
Here two (or more) children each have their own figure(s) and create scenes in which their figures are interacting with another child's figures. This is a highly advanced activity requiring sophisticated language, flexibility, improvisational skills, imagination, and strong social skills as the child must instantly adjust to

the other player's schema and ideas. Shared knowledge and nonverbal communication are very heavily used here. In short, I don't think it is a skill that we can teach our children until very late into a program. It is possible that your child will chronologically age out of this activity before you ever get around to it. I wouldn't bother teaching your child to memorize and act out a complicated social figurine play script because that activity does not go *anywhere* with peer play. Peers are not interested in puppeteering—they want to play.

At the risk of being sexist, I will say that many boys do not play with figurines extensively, even with action figures (G.I. Joe or WWF figures). I bring this up because I have seen play programs that spend a huge amount of time teaching a preschool child how to handle, manipulate, and talk for figurines in very complex and adult scenarios. Complex social figurine play is the highest level of *in vitro* pretend play and is not extensively done by every child. It is important to not spend a lot of time teaching a type of play that your child will not be able to use in social play situations.

Finally, beware of unconsciously limiting your child's imagination. If you are encouraging a child to talk for his figurine dog, then don't tell him his dog can't drive a car. Animals can't talk either, but somehow as adults, we are comfortable with that part of the fantasy, but not the driving part. This makes no sense whatsoever. Always think carefully about what you are teaching. There is no point in stopping play and explaining that dogs can't really drive, that they aren't people.

My son is now starting to play independently with toys in an appropriate way. He is picking up on things on his own now and I am totally excited! He is pretending his cars are going through the McDonald's drive though and puts the little toy aliens from Toy Story in a space ship and they fly to Mars. This play has just erupted in my son all of a sudden without any formal teaching and I am in complete shock. The other day, he set his stuffed animals in a circle and had a picnic of pretend foods and was feeding each of the animals pretend fruit and pizza.

Chapter 7
Games

- *Social Games and Classic Children's Games*
- *Music and Song Games*
- *Turn-Taking Games*
- *Board Games*

Games teach many skills, including strategy, physical fitness, perspective taking, social skills, mental skills, memory, sportsmanship, and ways of having just plain fun. When teaching game playing, start with physical social games rather than more complex board games. I have seen play programs in which children are taught to play complicated board games and yet never get a chance to play "Ring Around the Rosie."

Simple social games allow the child to use his or her body to play, in contrast to most board games, which emphasize sitting still for long periods and thinking. Physical games also have rather loose rules and don't emphasize winning. In fact, several rounds of the games can be played quickly so that many people might win in the course of a session of game playing. I think using short games is better starting out than playing a long game in which one person ultimately wins. Long games with only one winner are not very reinforcing to children, and they are too long for the attention spans of small children. I think turn-taking games and board games have been emphasized in Applied Behavioral Analysis (ABA) therapy in the past because it is easier to play these games with the only one or two adults who are usually available. However, if you can find some kids to play those outdoor, active games, I think game playing will become more fun and socializing for your child.

It might seem silly to write about the rules of these simple childhood games, but not everyone played all of these games. My consultant looked at me as if I were from another planet when I mentioned that I never played "Duck, Duck, Goose" as a child! Most of these physical social games have many regional variations or variations that you made up as a child. Feel free to teach these anyway you want.

SOCIAL GAMES AND CLASSIC CHILDREN'S GAMES

Social games are important for socialization, but how do you teach them with no other children available? Sometimes it is hard to find kids to play a pick-up game with a tutor and child. When you are first teaching a game, use the tutors and any person you can find who is willing—yourself, your neighbors, kids in the street, anyone. Adults may play most of these games. Just make sure you and your tutors are in good shape! You can play most of these games with just a few people. If you play in the front yard and make a lot of noise, other kids in the neighborhood might just show up. Or go to a playground with the child and tutor and try to get some kids to play these games with you. Don't be shy. Just say to some kids, "Hey, we are teaching our kid to play _____. Can you help us for five minutes?" Its amazing how helpful some kids can be if they are in the role of teacher. They might resist if you try to make them play the game for real. They might think it's for babies and not do it. But if you ask them to help you teach the game, they are more likely to play and have a blast doing it despite themselves.

Another option is to take advantage of any sort of day camp, YMCA camp, or family type children's activity program. If you talk to the director of these programs, they are often willing to accommodate a special needs child by allowing an aide to accompany him or her and provide some extra assistance. When we went to a family resort in Vermont, they assigned our son a special needs counselor who went with him through his day at camp. The counselor had the option of having our child play with the group or of pulling him out for one-on-one activities. After the first two very rough days, our child spent about half of his day participating in group activities and the other half in one-on-one hiking, swimming, and so forth.

These types of programs frequently use social games as a warm up to their more structured activities, and thus they serve as a good place to work on playing these games. Another advantage of these types of programs is that you don't burn out the peers and you aren't quite so concerned about how your child looks (you aren't going to see these people again usually). The first few times you do this sort of thing with your child, it might be very hard. The child might not make it through the whole day or even the first two hours. But if your child does well with structure and a routine, frequently each day gets a little better as he or she adjusts to the situation. Make sure your aides prompt the child to participate in the social games. Most preschool and day-care programs use these activities as well.

Choosing "It"
Early in teaching these games, you can pick "it" yourself or direct taking turns. At some point, however, you can teach the children how to pick "it" using an easy method. This method uses either of two rhymes that involve all players making fists and turning them sideways. Players stand in a circle with their fists in front of them. One person chants the rhymes while hitting the fists in sequence, one word for each fist. The fist that is hit on the last word is put behind the person's back. When both of a person's fists are behind the back, that person is out. The last person left is "it."

One Potato, Two Potato
One potato, two potato, three potato, four.
Five potato, six potato, seven potato, **more**.

Eenie, meenie, meinie, moe
Eenie, meenie, meinie, moe,
Catch a tiger by the toe.
If he hollers let him go,
Eenie, meenie, meinie, **moe**

Follow the Leader
This is a great game for observational learning. It needs to be made really fun, though. We did this first in therapy sessions, prompting our child through the motions. We had to have at least three people: a tutor, the child, and one other person. We dragged our older son into it most of the time. If he had friends over playing, we got them into the game too. First, you line up and identify the leader. The tutor usually asks, "Who's the leader?' and the first one in line says, "I am." Then the leader starts off all over the house and

outside in the yard, and everyone in line has to imitate him or her. The sillier the actions, the better. Our leaders crawled on their stomachs and banged on walls while running through the house. Add whooping, shouting, clapping, jumping off of chairs, and the game becomes really fun. At first, you will have to prompt your child to stay in line, watch the leader, and imitate everything he or she does. Put a tutor right behind your child to prompt him or her. Eventually your child will get to be the leader and make up actions. My child loved being in control and having us adults do crazy things: he started with just doing what the previous leader had done, but eventually he thought of some new actions himself.

This game can be tremendous fun if you move fast and do a lot of wild actions. Use this game to concentrate on nonverbal observational learning and following skills until they are rock solid.

Chase

This simple turn-taking game involves only two people. First the tutor "chases" the child, saying, "I'm gonna get you. I'm gonna get you!" and tickling the child if he or she catches the child. Prompt the child to say things like "You can't catch me!" Stay in a defined space so you don't end up chasing your child down the block. In the rooms of our downstairs we had a circular path that we used. After several turns of chasing the child, try to take a turn yourself. Say, "Now you chase me!" and start "running" slowly through the path your child has taken. Prompt him or her to follow you and try to tag you. Use hand gestures to indicate that he or she should follow you and say, "Chase me! Come and get me! I'm getting away!"

Having the child chase you, however, is not nearly as reinforcing to the child as your chasing him or her, so keep your turn short. You might also hold a reinforcer in your hand so that the child can get a reinforcer if he or she catches you. You don't have to take alternate turns at first. Give the child several turns between your turns and work up to alternate turn taking. Say, "Now its *my* turn." "Now its *your* turn."

"Duck, Duck, Goose"

In this game, kids sit down on chairs or on the floor in a circle facing each other. One person is "it" and walks around the circle. As "it" walks around, he or' she taps people's heads and says whether they are a "duck" or a "goose." Once "it" taps someone as the "goose," the "goose" gets up and tries to chase "it" around the circle. The goal for "goose" is to tag "it" before "it" is able sit down in the "goose's" spot.

If "it" is tagged, then he or she has to sit in the center of the circle until someone else is tagged to replace him or her. Goose becomes "it" for the next round.

"Hide and Seek"

Pick someone to be "it" (the person to seek). At the base "it" turns around and counts to a specified number with eyes closed while the rest of the players hide. Then "it" says, "Ready or not, here I come" and rushes to find everyone. The people hiding then try to run back to the base without getting tagged or else they are "it." If the person who is "it" doesn't tag someone in three tries, he or she gets to pick someone else to be "it"!

"Red Light, Green Light"
In this game, one person plays the "stoplight," and the rest of the players try to reach him or her first. At the start, all the children form a line about 15 feet away from the stoplight. In our version, the stoplight faces the line of people. My son found it hilarious watching a bunch of people running towards him. In a more advanced version, the stoplight faces away from the line of kids. The stoplight says "green light." At this point the kids are allowed to race towards the stoplight. At any point, the stoplight may say "red light!" or, if facing away, say, "red light" and turn around to face the line. If any of the kids are caught moving after this has occurred, they are out. While teaching this game, we didn't actually put anyone out for a long time. We just prompted our child (and others) to stop when "red light" was called out. Play resumes when the stoplight says "green light" or turns back around and says "green light." The stoplight wins if all the kids are out before anyone is able to touch him or her. Otherwise, the first player to touch the stoplight wins the game and earns the right to be "stoplight" for the next game.

We had a very steep driveway, and we played this game up the driveway. Running straight uphill made stopping easier and gave the children a workout. Have the players all take a turn playing the stoplight. Reinforce the concept of turn-taking by asking, "Whose turn is it?" and prompting the replies of: "It's my turn" or It's your turn."

"Tag"
The basic rules to "Tag" are simple. All you need is a group of kids and a decent size yard. Set some boundaries that the kids have to stay in. One person is designated as "it," and that person runs around and tries to tag someone else. If the person succeeds, the person he or she tags is now "it" and tries to chase everyone else. The game continues until everyone is exhausted or the tutors pass out!

"Hot Potato"
The children stand in a circle and pass a beanbag around the circle as music plays. When the music stops, the person holding the beanbag is out! Pretend the beanbag is a very hot potato and pass it quickly from one person to the next. Later, you can start throwing the beanbag back and forth while the music is playing, but I would wait until throwing and catching skills are good before attempting this variation.

"Crack the Whip"
This game can be played with just a few people, but the longer the train, the better. The players line up and hold hands to make a train of people. The first person in the line is the leader and the last person is the caboose. The leader starts running and everyone else follows, holding hands tight to keep from being thrown off the line. The leader makes sharp turns and runs at full speed to increase the force on the caboose. This is a lot of fun, but be prepared to get thrown off the line if you are on the end. The leader and caboose can use two hands to hold on to the one person they are connected to.

"Marco Polo"
This game is played in a swimming pool. All the players get in the pool and mark off a game boundary (usually the shallow end of the pool). The person chosen to be "it" closes his or her eyes and shouts "Marco," and all the others in the pool shout "Polo." The "Marco" shout and "Polo" response are repeated as "it" tries to tag one of the other players. "It" must play with his or her eyes closed, locating another player by sound only. Once tagged, that person becomes "it."

Fishing

Another simple pool "game" that my child liked to play was fishing. He would stand on the side of the pool and put the end of a "noodle" into the water. A child in the pool would grab the end of the noodle and my child would pull him or her to the side of the pool saying, "I've caught a fish."

"Treasure Hunt"

This game involves some advance preparation, but it's such a hit with kids that it's worth the extra effort. Before the playdate, decide where you want to kids to hunt, and then carefully hide little clues throughout the house. Write out your clues on note cards, and place them so that each clue will direct the children to the next one. For example, the word *couch* or a picture of a couch will lead the kids to the couch, where you've hidden a clue with the word *TV* or a picture of the TV on it. Label each clue with *one* child's name so that everyone gets a turn.

To start the game, hand the first clue to the first child. Have the child read the clue and find the next one (the other children will tag along and offer hints and suggestions). Once he or she has found the next clue, that clue is handed to the next child to read and follow.

Run the kids all over the place, until they find the treasure (I had a little "treasure chest" and put all sorts of stuff in it, including fake snakes and gold foil wrapped chocolate coins). You can make this game more complicated by adding prepositions to the instructions. For example, "Look inside the refrigerator." We played this game when the kids were dressing up as pirates, and they had a blast.

Animal Charades

Have a child come up to the front of the group. The tutor whispers the name of an animal to the child. He or she then acts out what the animal does (for example, the child might grunt like a pig or scratch the ground like a chicken). The rest of the children try to guess the name of the animal. To make it more fun, have the players make the animal's sound instead of calling out the name.

Charades

This game is described in Chapter 5.

"Twister"

Little kids love this game, especially when they get to fall all over each other. In the beginning, modify the game to say "hand" or "foot," leaving out the "left" and "right." Later, when the children know their lefts and rights, you can add that back in.

"Simon Says"

A child is chosen as "Simon." Everyone else stands in a line side by side. Simon calls out an action such as "Simon says, touch your nose." A nonverbal child may instead show a card (use pictures of people performing actions and touching body parts.). Everyone then performs the action. Prompt the children as necessary. There is no tricking in this version of the game. "Simon" calls out "Simon says" every time. Allow Simon a few turns and then switch players. In the traditional game, there is a "tricking" element that allows Simon to call out actions without saying, "Simon says." If a child performs the action at that point, he or she is out. Eventually, you can work up to playing the traditional game.

Easter Egg Hunt
Who says you can do this only at Easter? Put objects (candy, little toys, and stickers) in plastic Easter eggs and hide them all over the yard. The kids love to run and hunt them and find the surprises inside!

MUSIC AND SONG GAMES

"Ring Around the Rosie"
This game apparently originated during the Plague years and has a gruesome interpretation. However, it is still fun to play. The children form a circle holding hands and walk around singing:
Ring around the Rosie
Pocket full of posey
Ashes, Ashes,
We all fall down.

During the last line, all the kids fall down. Young children find this highly entertaining.

London Bridge Game
In this musical game, two children face each other and hold hands forming an arched bridge. Children in line pass under the bridge singing:

London Bridge is falling down,
Falling down, falling down.
London Bridge is falling down,
My fair Lady.

On "My fair lady," the arched arm bridge falls and captures a prisoner. The bridge then gently sways the prisoner back and forth while singing:

Take the key and lock her up.
Lock her up, lock her up.
Take the key and lock her up.
My fair lady.

Then the person is let out while the children sing the following verse.

Open up and let them out
Let them out
Let them out
Open up and let them out,
My fair lady.

And then the first verse is sung again, trapping another prisoner on "My fair lady."

Variation 1

The children forming the arch secretly decide who is silver and who is gold. At the end of the chorus, the prisoner is secretly asked, "Do you want to pay with silver or gold?" The prisoner then stands behind the child representing his choice. The game continues until all children have been captured. A tug-of-war between "gold" and "silver" ends the game.

Variation 2

This is the same as variation 1 through the choice of "silver" or "gold." At this point, the prisoner takes the place, in the bridge, of the child representing his choice. The child who was part of the bridge joins the line, and the game continues.

"Pop Goes the Weasel" Games

One child bounces a ball in rhythm while all the children sing the lyrics to the song. On the word *Pop*, he or she either passes or bounces the ball to another child, who repeats the game.

Lyrics

All around the cobbler's bench, the monkey chased the weasel.
The monkey thought 'twas all in fun. Pop goes the weasel!

To vary the game, have the children pass a ball around the circle while singing the song. On *Pop,* the child with the ball tosses it across the circle to another player, who begins the passing again.

"Hokey Pokey"

This song game is also taught in the songs program. Everyone stands in a circle to sing the song and make the appropriate body movements. Make sure a tutor is placed where the learning child can see him or her. Try to fade the tutor so that the child is watching a peer or someone else to follow the motions.

"Freeze Frame"

Have the children stand in a large room or wide-open space. Explain that when they hear the music, they can dance any way they want, but when the music stops, they must freeze immediately. Wait a few seconds to see if they can hold their positions, and then start over. You can also consider using a music video to do this so that when you hit the pause button, the people on the screen will freeze too!

Limbo

This version of the game doesn't require the children to bend backwards to get under the stick or rope. If you have the limbo music available, you can use it; otherwise you can just sing "*limbo, limbo, limbo*" to the limbo music tune as the kids file under a jump rope that is progressively lowered. The children can go under any way they want, and no one is out for touching the rope. Older kids, however, might want to try the traditional limbo maneuver as a challenge. We like to lower the rope until the kids have to scoot under it flat on their backs or stomachs! This game can get really silly.

Musical Follow the Leader

The children dance to music. You pick a leader, and the children have to follow whatever movement the leader does to the music. Have the leader face the group so they can see him or her. Every minute, change the leader.

Unmusical Chairs

Unlike the traditional version of the game, in this version no one is out. The children circle around a group of chairs while the music is playing. When the music stops, the children have to find a chair to sit on. However, you remove one chair each time, and the kids have to sit on each other's laps when the music stops. The object is to see if you can eventually pile everybody on one chair!

TURN-TAKING GAMES

The above social games, particularly games like "chase," can teach the rudiments of turn-taking. If you choose a strongly reinforcing activity, you might be able to teach turn-taking fairly fast. We taught turn-taking by making our children share a Nintendo game. A timer was set for the duration of each turn, and each child got to play until the timer went off. We then asked, "Whose turn is it?" This activity often degenerated into one or both children screaming in frustration, but the idea of turn-taking was learned solidly.

A less stressful way of teaching turn-taking is to make the children wait in short lines to do a very exciting activity. Here there is a strong physical prompt to wait one's turn because the child can't take a turn if someone is in front of him or her blocking access to the activity. You can teach turn-taking by having your child wait in line for something reinforcing, like jumping off a diving board or running through the sprinkler. Later you can have the children line up to hit a pinata or go down a slide. A game like London Bridge can teach walking and staying in lines to go under the bridge. Keep the lines short (3-4 kids at most) and let them take many turns while rotating them through the lines. This activity teaches the child that a short wait will pay off. If a child cuts in line, he or she must go to the back, of course.

Other activities that you can play that teach simple waiting in line and turn-taking include games such as:

➢ Ring toss
➢ Bean bag toss (use a box or a hula hoop target)
➢ Bowling games
➢ Horseshoes

BOARD GAMES

Even simple board games can be complicated for a young child. A game might require many separately taught targets to show the child how to spin a spinner, move a man on a path, manipulate the pieces, or place objects on a board. Break down each game as much as is required to teach the child how to play the game appropriately. In every game, the basics of game playing are introduced and reinforced. These include the concepts of turn-taking, winning, losing, sharing, and good sportsmanship. Board games are frequently too long for short attention spans, however, so I would hold off teaching them until your child is able to sit still and concentrate for the duration of the game.

Since you frequently have to break these games down into little parts, start with short, simple games like "Hungry Hungry Hippos" (my kid hated it, though), "Tic Tac Tony," "Barnyard Bingo," " Penguin Shuffle," and "Don't Break the Ice." Some of the popular preschool games are good, but a few may be too noisy and stimulating for some kids ("Lucky Ducks" caused us a lot of problems). Stay with games that are developmentally appropriate for your child. Traditional "Tic Tac Toe," for example, is very difficult for young children. My older typical son did not play this game until he was 8 years old. So I would not teach that game or any other game with strategy and blocking requirements early on.

After the child has learned to play a game, have the child play with the game with only a single peer, adult, or sibling for a long, long time. The dynamics of group board-game playing are too difficult for the child and the tutor to handle. Many typical children play board and other complex games with siblings and parents long before they start playing them with peers.

Board games are better left for 1:1 peer play rather than group peer play—at least in the beginning. In our playgroup, SPLAT was the biggest hit. This involved playdough and turn-taking, selecting cards, and moving along a path. Kids were more into this than other traditional games. Getting kids aged 4-6 through a whole game of CandyLand and Chutes and Ladders was tedious. They didn't have the patience if there was a group of kids. The board games like those are better left for 1:1 play rather than group play (except for SPLAT of course). What do you teach during board games? Well, you obviously teach winning, losing, being nice but not braggy about winning, being nice about losing, turn taking. You can teach your child to tell the other child it is his or her turn. Have a few playdates and look at the commenting. Half of our peers comment during board game play and half don't. They don't cheer each other on. They more or less laugh when the other person gets a bad turn. One kid would cheer for himself with "Yeah baby!" or something, so we taught similar phrases. First look what all the peers are saying. They aren't saying "nice try" to each other. Don't start teaching commenting skills without having observed typical kids in several different settings. Have a tutor sit back and watch and listen. They should write down the most common type of comments made by the peers, and then start teaching commenting. I never heard a single "nice try" or "way to go" from a peer. Most of it was rather egocentric.

Board Game Examples
This is a list of board type games we have taught during therapy. We studied each game and broke down each game into simple steps. We demonstrated each step to our child. We tried to emphasize turn-taking, winning, counting matches or points, watching the other players' moves, and following the rules. We had a hard time teaching the concept of 3-in-a-row for Tic-Tac-Toe. In retrospect, we should not have tried to teach that concept so early in game playing. Rather we should have concentrated on the social games that we played as my son enjoyed those very much. We took notes on each game after it was played to guide the next tutor. We worked on these games formally in therapy for two years.

➢ Winnie the Pooh Matching Game
➢ Household Lotto
➢ Don't Break the Ice
➢ The Maisy Game
➢ Animal Lotto
➢ Dinosaur Match

- Dinosaur Tic Tac Toe
- Air hockey
- Hungry, Hungry Hippos
- Original Memory Match
- Snail Pace Race
- Candyland
- Tic Tac Tony
- Hot potato
- Perfection
- Hi Ho Cherry-O
- Get Better Bear
- Secret Square
- Dominos (Maisy dominos)
- Tic Tac Toe (on white board)
- Chutes and Ladders (Snakes and Ladders)

GAMES TUTOR NOTES

Here are a few tutor note examples that are excerpted from our game program notes describing how specific games were played. Examples under each game start from the earliest experiences. These examples just cover a few of the games that we taught and only a few of the notes taken under each game.

Follow the Leader

He did 2 out of 7 actions. We played upstairs. Prompts were "No, look. Do what I do." Got the first 2 actions and attention bailed on the last 5. He got stuck on each action and didn't see the transition.

Prompted with "Watch Me," "Follow the Leader," and "Watch Julie."

He follows large gross motor motions (spinning and skipping) more than smaller gross motor (clapping and raising arms).

Better. I said, "Let's play Follow the Leader." He said, "You be the leader, I be the follow." Ha!

Winnie the Pooh Memory Matching Game

6 cards (3 matches.) Played game twice. First time was better than second. Need to work on turn-taking.

6 cards. Good, but I couldn't tell if he was looking at my mistakes or just remembering his mistakes. Went up to 8 cards and he made lots of mistakes.

10 cards. Pretty good work today. He won 2. I won 1. He worked off of my mistakes about 40% of the time.

10 cards. 2 games. We each won 1. Make sure he labels every card as it is turned over to help him pay attention. Make him verbalize the name of the characters and say, "it's [not] a match", etc. Make him count matches at the end and point out who the winner is.

10 cards. 2 games. Naming characters seems to help. Needed prompting approximately 95% of the time to name "Who is it?"

10 cards. 3 games. Still not naming characters without a prompt. Play of the game looks tons better.

8 cards. Total noncompliance.

10 cards. 2 games. Really super! Best time yet! Really looked at my mistakes and played off of them.

Started with 4 cards, then moved to 6. He threw the cards. He had a time-out.
Terrific game. Cheated once! Hooray! I think we can try all the cards.

24 cards. 2 games. He won one and I won one. Really terrific. Paid great attention and stayed with it. Seemed enthused to be playing.

18 cards. Noncompliance at first. Then he played very well. He won 6-3 and said, "I have 6 matches." Awesome.

34 cards (17 matches) = too many. Once we got down to about 9 matches left, he paid closer attention. He kept trying to find the match for one particular card and wouldn't move around. He was not paying attention to my mistakes.

A big fight from start to finish.

42 cards. 2 games. Eric won both games.

Red Light, Green Light

Great. He was stoplight the first time, then me, then Teresa. He did all games perfectly except the first: he didn't stop very well. We told him to come back and he did.

We played Red Light, Green Light. He started calling the lights. We played 6 or 7 times and he was having so much fun and giggling and smiling. Even when he didn't get to be the stoplight, no problems at all. Great!

Annakin (Eric) and Obi Wan Kenobi (me) played red light, green light. He did wonderfully and seemed to enjoy himself.

Dinosaur Tic Tac Toe/Tic Tac Toe

Worked on 3-in-a-row, you win! He did well—only missed 3-in-a-row once, but he mimicked my 3-in-a-row twice and I made him do a different 3-in-a-row the next three times.

Demonstrated 3-in-a-row, I win! Then he did 3-in-a-row I win. Then we played the game. He seemed to do fairly well. I didn't try to teach blocking. Once he got 2 in a row, I reminded him to try to get 3-in-a-row.

I showed him 3-in-a-row twice. He did the same one and I made him do a different one. We then played 2 games. We didn't block.

Not bad. Not great. He was focused on 3-in-a-row vs. taking turns. 4 games. Prompted "I win" and where to put the dinosaur for diagonal win.

Not good. Kept hitting Mom and me.

Good playing overall. He really wanted to get 3-in-a-row. He got upset the first time we played, though, because I blocked him and prompted him to go another way. The second game, he had no reaction when I blocked him and I prompted him to block me. Both times, he won, and I made him say it.

Pretty good. Eric once and I won once. I blocked him and prompted him to block me. Twice he tried to play more than one dinosaur. (I think he likes this game!)

Eric chose his color before each game. I don't think Eric understands what 3-in-a-row is—I think that he thinks if he has 3 on the board, he has 3-in-a-row and he wins. Maybe we should break this down somehow.

Played 2 times. He moved the bones (counters). He also said "I won, I get a bone." Doesn't get 3-in-a-row. 3 on the board = 3-in-a-row to Eric.

Still working on 3-in-a-row. I used a straight edge to help.

We played Tic Tac Toe on a white board. He really liked it. He wanted to be the O first, then he said "May I be the X with blue marker?" Then he said, "Look you have 3-in-a-row. We need to work on 3-in-a-row because he thought he could count all of his Xs.

Played well. He kept saying that he won when he had three that weren't in a row. The last time he won, we asked him why and he said, "because I got three in a row"

Played tic tac toe on the whiteboard. The first time I let him win. The second time when I got in his way, he tried to erase my X. He did understand that 3-not-in-a-row does not constitute 3-in-a-row, definitely an improvement.

We played tic tac toe. He played well the first two times, but the last time he wanted to erase my O because it was in his way. I wouldn't let him and finally got him to go somewhere else.

Played three times. He's getting better but he still has trouble blocking

Played on the whiteboard. The third game, Eric became very upset because I blocked him from getting 3-in-a-row. He said, "No, erase the X, and put it here" (indicating another spot).

Dinosaur Tic Tac Toe. Eric initiated playing on his own! Played 5 times. I spent each game trying to teach him to "block" me from getting 3-in-a-row. Had him visually scan the board and point to where he could block me. This seemed to help some. I made a big deal when I blocked him by saying "I'm gonna block you from 3-in-a-row"

We played on the whiteboard. I kept a tally of each time one of us won. He played four games. The first time, we filled up the board, and I asked him who won. He said, "Nobody". He won the second and third games by filling in the last square left—when I blocked him in both games, he asked, "Why did you do that?" I told him I blocked him because I wanted to win. When we finished the last game, I told him to look at the score and tell me who the big winner was. He said, "Eric, that's me!"

Game Sessions

Eric, Brother, and I played Candyland, Tic Tac Tony, Dino Match. Eric played and transitioned well. He tolerated it well when he was ready to switch games. Brother wanted to play "one more time."

Hi Ho Cherry-O, Candyland, the Maisy Game. Great Participation, great turn-taking. Good attention (lost him twice during Candyland).

We went outside to play games. I emphasized winning in everything we played (Tag, Treasure Hunt, Races, etc.) He answered correctly each time I asked him who won.

We played with Arthur's playset and then I tried to play Chutes and Ladders, but he wouldn't cooperate. He went into the closet and shut the door.

Lotto Games (Dinosaur, Animal, and Household)

Eric's choice. He took turn well, but didn't seem to get the idea of winning by filling up the card.

Animal Lotto. He picked out the game himself while I was sitting at the table. He asked me my name and then asked me if I wanted to play with him. He did very well with taking turns. After he filled his card, he said, "I won. I got all of my animals"

We played household lotto with D.W. and Arthur (dolls). He wanted each of them to have a card. I called out each card and he would raise the doll's hand and say "D.W. does" (have ___ card). Arthur won! We threw Arthur in the air back and forth and gave him high fives. Very fun for both of us!!

Played two games. Worked on the concepts of "My/Your card is full," "I/You win/won."

The Maisy Game

Eric always wants to be "Maisy goes to school." He wasn't too pleased that I didn't let him be that, but he got over it.

He had trouble attending half way through. He also had trouble with taking only 1 spin; he wanted to keep spinning the wheel.

I worked on taking turns, no cheating, and winning. Halfway through the game, he was set on getting "Maisy," and he became very upset when he spun another piece. I needed to do physical prompting to get him to spin appropriately and wait for his next turn.

Get Better Bear

Super! Much better at not counting the space he is sitting on as "one" when he begins to move. Starts with the next space at "one."

Eric's choice. He did a great job, but got a little restless towards the end. He was very interested in winning. He took turns well and played nicely.

By request again. Same problem. He wanted to be the shot and me to be the stethoscope. I told him I would be the thermometer and he started to argue. He got over it, but it looked like an "insistence of same" issue (he is always an item and his opponent is always the same item).

He played with Rachel and Anna. He had trouble with the concept of winning. He automatically said "I won" when asked even though he didn't. He wanted to "cheat" to get the correct number for a spin or to be ahead.

Hide and Seek

Eric's request. He sort of had the gist of it (two parts—the counter and the hider), but "tag, you're it"—he didn't get. He knew to go hide and it was away from me in another room.

About the same as before, but he's willing to play and learn! Had a ton of fun! Worked on tagging.

Continued working on "tag, you're it". A riot! We had the best time! He's doing better (variety) with hiding.

Twister

A riot! I didn't ask him for right/left. We had a lot of fun with Tori and Bobbie.

Hysterical. I think I had more fun. Two people works but more would be better.

Eric wanted this game to be over after a couple of rounds. It's real hard to do with two people; he had trouble differentiating between hand and feet.

Eric requested to play this game with Stephanie, Mom, and Anna. He was able to differentiate between left and right, but lost interest after three turns.

Chapter 8
Music

- *Materials*
- *Teaching Procedures*
- *Song Lists*

Singing, playing, and listening to music provide many skills for your child, such as language, gross and fine motor body movements, observational learning, and sequencing. But most importantly, they are opportunities for your child to experience the fun of social music making.

In addition, every preschool teacher knows that singing can organize a chaotic roomful of children. Young children have not developed the organizational abilities to use time and space boundaries as adults do. Songs can organize time into small chunks through rhythm and words, and this organization helps children develop the ability to anticipate. That's why so many teachers use music as a transitional tool—and why there are so many clean-up songs, hello songs, and end-of-day songs. You can use these types of transitional songs in therapy and during the day at home to get your child used to singing them in preschool.

You can teach music anywhere and anytime. We all know dozens of songs that we sang at home, in school, and in camp—from the sacred to the profane and just plain silly! Sing with your child throughout all the day: in the morning getting dressed, in the car, and at night as a bedtime ritual.

MATERIALS

Song Lyric Book
You will need a ready reference for lyrics to carry with you and use in therapy. I made up a separate song lyric book in a small, soft-sided, 3-ring binder. I copied lyrics with instructions for the hand and body movements from the internet (there are many websites dedicated to children's song lyrics), from Wee Sing songbooks, and other sources and laminated them. The tutors wrote out some of the lyrics by hand as they recalled them or after our child heard them at school. Hand and body motions were written out and demonstrated in team meetings if necessary. This binder then served as a reference for the tutors. The book should be large enough to hold all the songs, but small enough to carry around in the car or on trips.

Music Tapes
My child really responded to song tapes, especially "children's favorites" tapes and Wee Sing tapes. He and the tutor sang the songs to the tapes as they were played. We had a small collection of these and a tape recorder available in his room and in the car.

Music Video Tapes

Several videos have children singing basic children's songs. My son really enjoyed these as well. They are inexpensive or can be rented cheaply from the video store. Barney tapes have many traditional songs that you can teach—although Barney changes the words sometimes to fit the occasion and these changes can be confusing for your child. On the other hand, these variations can be helpful. My child learned to make up his own lyrics to popular song tunes, and he enjoyed the seasonal variations that his teachers came up with (for example, "Mr. Turkey" sung to the tune of "Frere Jacques.") The *Kidsongs* videos are also very good and cover many of the classic songs of childhood. The problem with videos is that the child can't watch the tutor while he or she is watching the video, but videos can provide your child with the words and body movements so that he or she can practice later with the tutor and other children.

People!

Teach everyone in your child's life the songs so they can be sung anywhere, anytime. Songs should be incorporated all day—wake-up songs in the morning with all of your kids, during play with playdates and tutors, during therapy, in the car, with groups of kids at anyone's house. Pick a song and sing it, or have other kids pick a song for everyone to sing. Try to teach some of the songs that are sung in parts (one person sings one part and another person sings a refrain or reply).

Do not be afraid to sing! You need to overcome your own fear of singing poorly and belt out the songs. Really ham up those body movements as well so your child can learn!

TEACHING PROCEDURES

You can start by just letting the child listen to you sing by yourself or along with a cassette player tape or video. Then start singing the song and doing the motions while the child is watching you. Work on having the child imitate the motions as you sing. Then try to get him or her to fill in the last word of a phrase.

Start with a repetitive song like "Wheels on the Bus" that has hand motions.
Teach the first lyric by dropping off the end of the line and see if your child will fill in the blank. "The wheels on the bus go round and _____."

Prompt the child to add the right word. Then work backwards to having him or her sing the whole phrase. Continue to break down the song in this way until the child can sing and move to the music with you. While the child is learning the song, he or she can listen to it on the tape or video at any time out of therapy to reinforce the words and music. Eventually you and the child should be singing and doing the hand motions together or to a recorded source.

This teaching can be an arduous process in therapy. Start with one song and really work on teaching it. At the same time, introduce all sorts of additional songs throughout the day and expose the child to singing via tapes, videos, and your own songs. However, expect him or her to participate in therapy to only the one song he or she is learning. If the child sings otherwise, fantastic! But don't make singing outside of therapy too work-like. Singing is supposed to be fun.

We had trouble getting our child to sing so that he could be heard. I also think he had some auditory processing problems and would totally garble words to the music (I think he was just singing what he "heard"). We did try to clean up the words but didn't get super exact with him; we were more interested in his singing and participating than in his getting every single word right. Besides, everyone knows that children frequently garble words to songs, and there are humorous books and collections of how normal children have messed up the words to songs. We concentrated on the fun of singing and music rather than on precision.

Interactive songs where one line is sung by one person and the next by the next person are great for teaching back and forth "conversational" style. These songs include "Down by the Bay" and "Hole in the Ground."

SONG LISTS

The Songs We Taught in Therapy
This list is of the actual songs we taught our child in therapy. His preschool teachers also taught him variations to common songs. These variations were usually related to holidays.

"Wheels on the Bus"
- Wipers
- Horn
- Doors
- Babies
- Parents
- Blinkers

"This Old Man"
- Thumb
- Shoe
- Knee
- Door
- Hive
- Sticks
- Heaven
- Gate
- Spine
- Once again

"Barney Song"
"Daisy"
"Patty Cake"
"Thumbkin"
"Hey, Mr. Knickerbocker"
"I'm a Little Teapot"
"Twinkle, Twinkle, Little Star"

"Mr. Sun"
"Firetruck"
"Skit Marink a Dink"
"Itsy Bitsy Spider"
"Old MacDonald"
>	Chick
>	Ducks
>	Cow
>	Turkey
>	Pig
>	Donkey

"Down by the Bay"
"Sing a Rainbow"
"Sally the Camel"
"Happy Birthday"
Holiday and Seasonal Songs
"Hole in the Ground"
"Elephant Song"
"Baby Bumblebee"
"Working on the Railroad"
"It's a Small World"
"Ants Go Marching"
"Oh You Can't Get to Heaven"
"Jesus Loves Me"
"Apples and Bananas"
"John Jacob"
"Hokey Pokey"
"Raindrop Song"
"Boa Constrictor"
"Roll Over"
"London Bridge"

Here are lists of classic preschool and early school years songs that you can also consider for your program. Lyrics are widely available on the Internet or in childhood song collections (for example, the Wee Sing series)

PRESCHOOL SONGS
"Aiken Drum"
"Alouette"
"Baa Baa Black Sheep"
"Bingo"
"Did You Ever See a Lassie"
"Eencey Weencey Spider"
"Here We Go 'Round the Mulberry Bush"
"Hole in the Bucket"

"The Hokey Pokey"
"If You're Happy and You Know It"
"I've Been Working on the Railroad"
"Mary Had a Little Lamb"
"The Muffin Man"
"Oats, Peas, Beans and Barley Grow"
"Oh, Dear, What Can the Matter Be?"
"Old MacDonald Had a Farm"
"Pop Goes the Weasel"
"Ring Around the Rosie"
"Row, Row, Row Your Boat"
"Sing a Song of Sixpence"
"Three Blind Mice"
"A Tisket, a Tasket"
"Twinkle, Twinkle, Little Star"
"The Wheels on the Bus"

EARLY SCHOOL YEARS
"The Ants Go Marching"
"Baby Beluga"
"The Bear Went Over the Mountain"
"Clementine"
"Down by the Riverside"
"Frère Jacques"
"He's Got the Whole World in His Hand"
"Home on the Range"
"If I Had a Hammer"
"Little Bunny Foo Foo"
"London Bridge Is Falling Down"
"Michael, Row the Boat Ashore"
"Mister Frog Went a Courtin'"
"Oh Susanna"
"On Top of Spaghetti"
"Puff the Magic Dragon"
"Rise and Shine"
"She'll Be Comin' Round the Mountain"
"Simple Gifts"
"Skip, Skip, Skip to My Lou"
"Take Me Out to the Ball Game"
"This Land Is Your Land"
"This Little Light of Mine"
"When Johnny Comes Marching Home"
"Yankee Doodle"
"You Are My Sunshine"

Music Games—See Games (Chapter 7)

Chapter 9
Sensory and Physical Play

- *Playdough and Clay*
- *Putty and Slime*
- *Gross Motor Play Activities*
- *Ball Play and Sports*

PLAYDOUGH AND CLAY

Playdough and clay are wonderful materials for tactile and sensory play. In addition to providing some pleasant sensory experiences, tactile activities are a great way to strengthen fine motor skills. Making items, decorating them, and pretending with them can enhance creativity.

There are many different types of clay. Oil-based clays and polymer modeling clay usually won't dry out. Water-based clays will dry out, and some clays need to be baked to be hardened well. Play clays like playdough are soft and easy to manipulate. It's best to work with a soft play clay like playdough when your child is young. When he or she is older, you can make permanent creations from water-based clay by air-drying or baking them and then painting them. Older children will also enjoy working with the nondrying polymer clays, which are harder to manipulate and shape but may be used to create complex designs.

Several types of commercial playdough are available such as Playdoh and Crayola Dough. Commercial clays are available which can be air-dried (Crayola Model Magic) or baked. Polymer non-drying modeling clays are made by several companies and are sold at craft and art supply stores. For a change from the commercial products, try some homemade playdough and clay. Homemade playdough and clays are relatively easy to make, and children enjoy mixing and kneading the dough.

HOMEMADE PLAYDOUGH RECIPES

Playdough is a soft play type of modeling clay. It is the type of clay used typically in preschool and kindergarten. The advantages of this soft clay are that it is easy to manipulate and can be used over and over. However, it will dry out if not kept in an airtight container. Dried playdough is too brittle to be used for permanent creations.

Playdough. The following is my favorite recipe for playdough. It seems to have the best consistency and keeps for a long time.

1 c. flour
1/2 c. salt

2 tbsp. cream of tarter
1 c. water
1 tbsp. vegetable oil
5 to 6 drops food coloring, optional

Mix the ingredients and heat the mixture over medium heat. Stir it until a ball forms. Let it cool and knead it until it is smooth. The secret to a successful playdough is in the kneading. The more you knead it, the smoother it will be. Keep the playdough in an airtight container or zip lock bag.

Another way to color the playdough is to put some plain playdough in a plastic bag, let children add the food coloring to the bag, close it, and let them knead the color into the dough.

Kool-Aid Playdough. This variation creates colored playdough with distinctive scents.
2 c. all-purpose flour
1/2 c. salt
2 packages unsweetened Kool-Aid
4 tsp. cream of tartar
2 c. water
2 tbsp. oil

Mix the ingredients in a large pan. Cook and stir the mixture over low heat until it thickens and the bottom is just starting to crust up, about 15 minutes. The dough will be stiff and hard at this point. Turn the dough out onto a large cookie sheet and let it cool. When it is cool, knead it until it is smooth. Store it in a covered container or zip lock bag.

Uncooked Playdough. When you don't have time to cook the playdough, try this uncooked variation.
3 c. flour
1/4 c. salt
1 c. water
1 tbsp. oil
Food coloring

Mix the flour and salt. Gradually add the water, food coloring, and oil. Add more water if the mixture is too stiff; add more flour if it is too sticky. Let the children help with the mixing and measuring. Knead the dough until it is smooth. Keep the dough stored in plastic bags or a covered container.

Homemade Clays that Harden
These clays will harden by air-drying or baking. They are suitable for making permanent creations. The child may wish to paint the clay when it has dried.

Play Clay. This simple clay will harden after a day or two of air-drying.
1 c. cornstarch
2 c. baking soda
1 1/4 c. water

Combine the cornstarch and baking soda thoroughly in a saucepan. Mix in the water. Bring the mixture to a boil over medium heat, stirring constantly, until it reaches a moist, mashed-potato consistency. Remove it immediately from the heat. Turn it out on a plate and cover it with a damp cloth until it is cool. When it is easy to handle, knead it like dough. Shape the clay as desired or store it in a tightly closed plastic bag for later use. After air-drying, the clay objects may be left white or painted. For colored play clay, add a few drops of food coloring or tempera paint powder to the water before it is mixed in with the starch and soda.

Salt Clay. This clay contains salt and hardens after a few days of air-drying.
1 c. water
1/2 c. flour
1 c. salt
Food coloring (optional)

Mix all ingredients in a saucepan. Add the food coloring if desired. Stir the mixture over low heat. When it is thick and rubbery remove it from the heat. Spoon the clay onto a floured sheet of waxed paper, and roll it out. Cut out or model objects. Air-dry the objects for a few days to harden them. Store the dough in an airtight container to prevent drying.

Bakeable Salt Clay. This salt clay requires baking to be thoroughly hardened.
2 c. flour
1 c. salt
1 to 1 1/2 c. cold water
2 tbsp. cooking oil
Food coloring, optional

Stir the ingredients together. Knead the mixture well until it forms a soft ball. Create the shapes you want and place them on a baking tray lined with aluminum foil. Bake the creations in the oven at 300 degrees until hard (about one hour). Paint the objects as desired. A finishing coat of shellac or clear acrylic will make your salt clay products last longer.

Sand Clay. This unusual clay uses sand as the base and creates hard stone-like sculptures when air-dried
2 c. sand (plain or colored)
1 c. cornstarch
2 tsp. alum
1-1/2 c. water
Food coloring, optional

Mix the ingredients in a saucepan. Stir the mixture constantly while cooking over medium heat. Remove it from the heat when the mixture thickens and becomes hard to stir. Cool 10 - 15 minutes. After making clay objects or cut-outs, air-dry them for several days. Paint the objects if desired. Store the left over clay in an air-tight container to prevent drying. To produce lightly colored objects, use fine white sand.

TOOLS FOR CLAY AND PLAYDOUGH CREATIONS
Early play with clay and playdough requires only a pair of hands. Manipulating the clay with your hands will warm it up, making it easier to manipulate. You can use your fingers to poke dents and holes in the

clay. You can make little lines and cuts with your fingernails. For more advanced play, keep a box of supplies on hand. Tools helpful for working with clay and playdough include:

Work board. Use a smooth hard surface like a dry erase white board. (Remember that some clays are oily)

Plastic knife. Use this to cut the clay or flatten small pieces.

Commercial modeling tool sets, Playdoh factory equipment, or Crayola Dough Fun Shapers

Tinker Toy Sticks. Use these or short dowel rods as small rolling pins. The ends of the sticks can be used to poke holes and make dents

Toothpicks and paperclips. Use the tips of the paper clips and toothpicks to make designs in the clay. Toothpicks are also helpful to attach pieces of clay together to make arms and legs or to add support to thin pieces.

Kitchen equipment

BASIC SHAPES

These simple shapes can be taught imitatively. As you are making the shapes with the child, label them so that later when you are helping a child create more complex creations, you can use the same names to describe the parts of the object.

Ball. Roll a lump of clay between your two palms until it becomes a ball. Continue to roll it around until it is smooth and uniform in shape. Have the child make balls of different sizes.

Pancake. Start with a rough ball of clay and flatten it on the board with the palm of your hand or flatten between your two palms. Smooth over any rough edges with your fingers. Have the child make thin and thick pancakes.

Snake. Roll a piece of clay back and forth between your palms or on a board until it takes on a noodle or snake shape. Have the child make short thick snakes and long thin snakes. Experiment with different amounts of clay to make very small worms and large thick snakes.

Log. Start to roll a lump of clay back and forth on the board or between your palms. Stop while the clay is still short and thick like a log.

Cylinder. Take a log and cut off the tapered ends with a knife. Or roll out a short fat log and press the ends on the board to flatten them.

Brick. On the board, place a log and then flatten the top and bottom with another small board. Turn the log and press the other two sides the same way.

Design Ideas

I've listed some examples of different creations the child can make. For other ideas, copy the examples found on the boxes of Playdoh and modeling clay. Cut the pictures out and use them as guides while you are playing. Other sources for ideas include clay-modeling books and websites dedicated to clay modeling. These sources often have very advanced designs, however, and for a preschool child I would stick with the basics. Once you have created a design, be sure to play with the creation. For example, once the child has created some food items, use them in a Pretend play center kitchen or on a pretend picnic. Also show the child how to experiment with mixing colors. Start by mixing two of the primary dough colors (red, blue and yellow) to make secondary colors (orange, green, and purple).

EXAMPLES OF CLAY AND PLAYDOUGH DESIGNS

Food Creations
*Pancake (*put a thin irregularly shaped pancake on top for syrup*)*
*Egg (*decorate like an Easter Egg*)*
*Noodles and Meatballs (*make a pile of thin snakes and top with balls*)*
Hamburger (two pancakes and a patty of another color)
Sausages (make several logs of the same size)
Hot dog (sausage and pancake—fold a pancake into a hot dog bun)
Dough (use a rolling pin to roll out the clay like dough)
Cookies (use cookie cutters to make cookies)
Donuts and bagels (attach the head and tail of a thick snake)
Fruits and fruit bowl (banana, apple, pear, plum, strawberry, and berries)

Animals
Playdough bugs. Make a bug's body (a slightly flattened log or ball) and use toothpicks or pipe cleaners cut about 3 inches long to make legs and antennae. Or make the legs out of clay.
Snakes. After making a snake, decorate it with little dots and stripes. You can also add little dots for eyes and a little thin red snake for a tongue!
Spider. Flatten the bottom of a ball of clay on the board to make the spider's body.. Use a smaller ball for the head, and add some eyes and eight thin little snakes for legs.
Turtle. Use a thick pancake for the bottom of the shell. Add the legs, a head, and a tail overlapping the ends of these parts over the bottom pancake. Then put another pancake on top. Press the edges of the top pancake down and over to touch the bottom pancake. Draw a shell design with the end of a toothpick, a paperclip, or your fingernails.

People
Faces. Make normal faces and clown faces.
Snowman. Make this the way you would make a real one. You can use toothpick arms, a ribbon scarf, and other little details, as you are able.
Person. Use a slightly flattened cylinder for the body. To make legs, roll a thick snake and fold it in half. Press the fold into the bottom of the body. Attach some arms and a head.
Person in bed. Make a thin slab, and put a person on the slab. Add a thin top slab.

Other Objects
Car. Make a thin brick for the bottom of the car and put a smaller brick on top to make the passenger compartment. Attach four wheels made from flattened balls. You can add other parts like headlights and bumpers made from snakes. To make a convertible, scoop out the inside of the car, and then add a steering wheel.
Flowers. Make a snake stem and flat leaves. Make the flowers from small pancakes and decorate them with little dots. You can also make several small pedals and attach them to the stems.
Jewelry Beads. Roll pieces of dough into small balls or cut a snake into equal size pieces. Use a pencil, a paper clip, or a nail to open holes for stringing. To make permanent jewelry, use clay that can be dried. Allow the beads to dry thoroughly before stringing them on yarn.
Ornaments. Combine dough beads, snakes, and other shapes to make relief designs, ornaments, and pen-

dants. Or roll out the clay and use plastic knives and cookie cutters. Open a hole at the top of the ornaments and pendants. After the piece dries, string it on ribbon or yarn.

Pots. Make several snakes. Join the ends of each snake to make a loop. Stack the loops compactly to make pots and lids.

PUTTY AND SLIME

There is something irresistible about playing with Slime, Silly Putty, and GAK. These commercial tactile sensory stimulants are designed to be squashed through the fingers in an unstructured way. They have no real purpose other than to provide a sensory experience, but they are fun and children love them. After my son left a wad of Silly Putty at my office once, I found myself playing with it between seeing patients. The commercial slime and putty products are fun and are inexpensive, but the recipes below are easy to follow and also provide some very interesting sensory experiences.

Cornstarch Slime

This stuff is *wild*! You should definitely try it yourself for a really bizarre sensory experience. There are only two ingredients, dry cornstarch and water (food coloring is optional and is *not* recommended on your first attempt). When mixing the two ingredients, realize that the lines are very thin between dry cornstarch, slime, and cloudy white starch water. Mix the ingredients slowly and add the water only a little at a time. Start with two parts cornstarch in a bowl. Slowly, add one part water, mixing with your fingers to get all of the powder wet. Have more water handy, and drop in a little at a time, mixing as you go. It will take much less water than you might think to change the consistency, so add only a few drops at a time. You will know when it is the right amount, as the wet powder will stick together and suddenly start behaving very oddly. This slime has some weird properties. It will "melt" between your fingers, but let it sit just a minute and it turns to concrete, melting again once you pick it up.

Slime

This concoction is another very interesting sensory experience. You can store this in an airtight container for later use.

2 c. white glue
1 1/2 c. water
Food coloring
1 tsp. Borax
1/2 c. water

Mix the glue, 1 ½ c. water and the food coloring until the mixture is no longer sticky. Separately dissolve the Borax and ½ c. water. Add this mixture to the glue solution. With clean hands, knead this slime to get it to mix. This will take about 10 minutes. If you desire a looser, slimier texture, add a bit more water and knead it in.

Fun Putty
This putty also should be stored in an airtight container. Mix the following ingredients together well:

1/2 c. white glue
1/4 c. liquid starch
(or 2 parts glue to 1 part starch)
Mix the ingredients together well. Store in an airtight container

GROSS MOTOR PLAY ACTIVITIES

Gross motor activities work on large body movements and help develop motor tone and coordination. While they are important for exercise and exploration, gross motor activities can also provide fun and peer play without the need for sophisticated language. An adult playing with the child should be able to do all of these activities without difficulty. The equipment for some of these activities can be found at small carnivals, playgrounds, commercial play sites (for example, Chuckie Cheese). Try to find a site that lets an adult play on the equipment as well.

I'm focusing more on sports and physical type toys now because they're easier to play without language. Having the swing set and trampoline in the yard has helped because other kids come to use the equipment when our son is playing.

Ball Box. Fill a small wading pool with the plastic colored balls like the ones they use at play parks and McDonald's. Or better yet, take the child to one of the playgrounds with the giant ball pits. Get into the ball pit yourself so you can show the child such activities as throwing the child into the balls, jumping into the balls, throwing the balls, getting buried, digging, and falling.

Obstacle Course. Kids love to climb through big cardboard box mazes or the large playground obstacle courses. Create an obstacle course at home using chairs and other household items. The child can crawl under a table or over a "mountain" of pillows. He or she can step in and out of a tire, on and off of a stool, or through the rungs of a ladder. Start simple and then make the course more complex. Incorporate crawling, climbing, jumping, tunneling, and sliding.

Playground Equipment. Teach the child to slide, swing, climb, and seesaw using home or community playground equipment. To teach the child to swing from bar to bar on a Jungle Gym, hold the child around the waist as he or she swings from bar to bar. Alternatively, put the child on your back and shoulders.

Balance beam. Some playgrounds have very low balance beams only a few inches off the ground. You can also set up narrow boards on the ground at home. Work on walking straight, walking sideways, and walking backwards on the beam. Try playing "Follow the Leader" with this activity.

Jumping. Start by teaching the child to jump off of a curb. Progress to having the child jump off a step and then to jump off of progressively higher points.

Trampolines. Jumping on small compact trampolines provides some exercise while improving coordination. The enclosed air-filled jumping structures are also great; they are extremely fun and safe, although most will not let allow an adult play inside. These can be found at small carnivals and playgrounds. Large backyard trampolines can provide a wonderful playdate activity and draw in other interested children from the neighborhood.

Walks. At one time, tutors would take my child for a 15-minute walk in the neighborhood. Learning not to run off was actually the purpose of the walk, but the exercise was helpful for my child, providing physical relief from therapy and some fresh air. The tutor worked very hard to keep my child from running off while teaching him to stay with her during the walk. The tutor tried to walk as fast as possible to give my child a workout. Sometimes, the tutors worked on therapy programs, asking questions and doing some initiative gross motor activities, but usually the tutor and my child just enjoyed the walk. Walking with the child is a good habit to develop for later childhood.

Hopper Balls. These large balls are designed for the child to sit on and bounce around. They have a handle that the child can hold on to as he or she jumps around. Be sure to find one that will be large enough for the tutor as well. Later, you can have hopper ball races with peers.

Piggyback rides. Piggyback rides give a harder workout for the adult than the child, but they are important for teaching upper body balance. At the pool, put the child on your shoulders.

Pile driver. Turn the child upside down and hold him or her firmly around the waist and legs. Shake him up and down like you are using his head as a pile driver (do this on the carpet and be careful!).

Wheelbarrow. Hold the child's legs in the air while he or she is using the arms to support his upper body. The child should try to walk on his or her hands while you are holding his or her legs in the air. If this is too hard for the child, get a large, firm beach ball and have the child roll forward onto his or her arms as you help him or her balance. Progressively have the child put more weight on the arms until he or she can walk on the hands. Later, the child and his peers can have a wheelbarrow race.

Balloon Play. Balloons can provide entertaining gross motor activities. Games such as trying to keep a balloon from touching the ground, playing balloon volleyball, and using the balloon as a punching ball, are not only fun but provide additional skills.

Racing. Teach the child to run a race to a specified point. You can expand this activity from a game of chase. Start with teaching the child to run to a discrete finish point. You can use a visual cue, like a line to cross or a suspended rope, but a stationary object (like the mailbox) is usually easier to start with. Prompt the child to run with you to the specified point, teaching him or her to stop at the endpoint. Identify the "winner" of the race every time. Eventually you can teach the child to line up at a starting point with a group of peers and to wait for a starting signal to begin. To improve the motivation to win, give the winner of every race a reinforcer. The idea that "winning" in and of itself is reinforcing takes some time for children to accept.

Other ideas for fun gross motor activities include:
- Pogo sticks
- Scooters
- Dizzy disc and Sit and spin
- Ribbon sticks
- Stomper stilts
- Sword and Pillow fights
- Arm and thumb wrestling

BALL PLAY

> *I think that spending time on play skills in which the child just doesn't have an interest is a waste of time. I pushed learning to build with Legos, and while it was great for fine motor development, my daughter never took to it. However, I am glad that we stuck with throwing and catching a ball because that is something that we can now use with her.*

Ball play involves basic skills that can advance in complexity as the child gets older. Team sport skills such as batting and running bases can be reserved for later programs, but playing "Catch" is a relatively slow, deliberate, social activity that doesn't require a lot of conversation and should be taught early. Note that the game itself is called "Catch," not "Throw," characterizing it as a reciprocal activity between two players. The receptive and reciprocal nature of this activity accounts for its status as a highly rated bonding activity, particularly for fathers and sons.

Ball play should start with the child throwing a ball without direction. This ball should be small enough for the child to hold it in his or her hand. A ball pit is a good place to start this activity as the ball does not need to be thrown in any particular direction. Later you can work up to having the child throw the ball in a particular direction, perhaps into a large box or at a very large target. Larger balls that require two hands to throw should also be introduced at this point. The child can throw these balls into a large box on the ground. Eventually you can set the box at higher levels, working towards throwing the ball into a basketball type goal. Other items can be used to teach throwing as well. Beanbag toss, ring games, and darts all teach the child to throw at a target. Eventually, you can work on having the child throw the ball to you. From there, you can develop the game of "catch" with the child.

> *I would have searched high and low for at least one male tutor. We hired one temporarily for the summer and had wonderful results. We didn't use him for the traditional ABA programs. We used him for coordination programs, sports programs, and downtime play. My son actually liked playing ball with this tutor. He imitated the male tutor's more "manly" ball-throwing style. Most of my tutors are "girly" girls. I sat one day and watched a well-intentioned female tutor work on a gross motor program with my son. She was wearing sandals and was trying to kick a soccer ball. She kept her hands up in the air and sort of flapped them whenever she kicked. Needless to say, our son imitated right after her!*

Teaching the child to catch uses a different approach. When you begin to teach the child to catch the ball, start with *bouncing* the ball to him or her. Use a larger ball such as a beach ball. Bounce the ball to the child and teach him or her to catch it with two hands. A child can usually catch a bounced ball before he or she can catch a thrown ball. Teach the child to bounce the ball back to you. This skill (bouncing a ball back and forth) is used in such games such as foursquare and the "Pop Goes the Weasel" musical game (see Chapter 7). Eventually, you will teach the child to catch a thrown ball. Start again with a large ball that can be caught with two hands and progress to smaller balls that can be caught with one hand.

Sports Activities

For older school-aged children, sports activities become more prominent. These skills, which include bike riding, skating, swimming, and jumping rope, become very important activities for peer play. They can be very difficult to teach as to master them requires persistence and motivation in addition to repeated practice. In these activities you might have to employ a class or tutor for one on one instruction.

Our son is older now at age 12. It takes a good deal of time to teach him play skills so we choose carefully. We taught long-term projects; the games and activities that won't be outgrown and abandoned. We looked at what peers were playing then looked ahead to see what they were playing in 1 or 2 years. We studied the school playground and did interest surveys of peers. Activities we taught were either long-term group activities, good leisure skills and/or good exercise. We first taught appropriate play on all equipment at the school playground, then basketball, swimming, Uno, biking, hiking and bowling. These activities are popular in our area.

Chapter 10
Water and Sand Play

- *Water Play*
- *Exploratory Water Play*
- *Water Painting and Art Activities*
- *Water Pretend Activities*
- *Social Water Games*
- *Water Parks*
- *Sand Play*
- *Sand Play Materials*
- *Sensory Activities and Exploratory Play*
- *Sand Pretend Activities*
- *Sand Building*
- *Sand Art*
- *Sensory Box*

Both sand and water are excellent and enjoyable materials for play. They provide pleasant sensory and physical experiences while you are teaching important playskills involving pretend play, building with manipulatives, physical skills, and games.

WATER PLAY

Children love water and water play. Every time I set up a Slip and Slide in our front yard, the neighborhood kids came running to join in the fun! I strongly recommend that you put your own swimsuit on and join in all the fun of these activities.

A wide variety of sources for water and water play are available such as:

- Wading Pools
- Garden hoses
- Water sprinklers
- Large community pools
- Educational water tables, washtubs, and dishpans
- Bathtubs, showers, whirlpools, jacuzzis
- Water parks

Don't limit yourself to the pool or garden hose, however. Make sure your child has the experience of exploring natural bodies of water such as:

➢ Rivers
➢ Ocean
➢ Lakes
➢ Ponds
➢ Puddles
➢ Rainstorms

EXPLORATORY WATER PLAY

Begin water exploration by letting your child fill and empty containers and pour from one container to another. Pour "tea" into cups from pitchers and "water" the plants. Let your child practice pouring water from container to container. Use different settings—a wading pool, a swimming pool, buckets, pans, and natural sources of water. Bring your water play materials to a public pool, and let your child play with them in the children's pool. Have your child share his or her materials with the other children.

Have your child retrieve objects in the water with tongs, aquarium nets, scoops, and fingers. Work out the child's small muscles by squeezing squirt bottles and spraying misters. Squeeze bottles of water and misters offer a variety of play opportunities. Demonstrate the ways to squirt long or short distances. Or, show the child how to create designs on the water's surface or on the driveway. Explore the many uses of water pistols, spray bottles, and misters. Put out paper cups on a table and get the child to try to shoot them and knock them over. Sponges are also fun to squeeze and fill with water. Have the child sop up water from one place with a sponge and squeeze it into a container. "Paint" with the sponges, and throw them to make a pleasing sound and sight as they hit the pavement or side of the house. Show the child the various ways to splash the water. Splashing can be a fun reciprocal activity if it doesn't get out of hand.

Other fun exploratory activities include:

Rain Play. If there is no lightning, take the child out in the rain. Do everything you would normally do if it were not raining. Go for a walk, play ball, or just twirl around in the rain. Being in the rain is a lot more fun than most people realize.

Water Sprinkler. Just let the kids run through the sprinklers. This simple activity is very entertaining for children. Try playing "follow the leader" through the sprinklers.

Water Showers. Take a large beach umbrella and tape a garden hose on the inside of it with the nozzle pointing up so that all the water rains down on the inside of it.

Bubbles. Bubbles are always a favorite. It's difficult to teach a young child how to blow them with his or her mouth, so use bubble blowers and large loops so the child can create bubbles easily. As you go along, work on teaching the child to blow bubbles, but let the child enjoy them first.

Bubble Soap. Use this recipe to make a large batch of bubble soap for use by several children.

1 gallon water (use distilled if your water is hard)

1 cup Joy or Dawn liquid dish washing soap

1/8 cup glycerin

Fill a bucket or container with water. Add the liquid soap and glycerin. Stir gently.

Bubble Pool. Add bubble soap to an empty children's wading pool. Add various bubble toys like empty bottles, straws, hoops, string, coat hangers bent into circles, and plastic bubble toys. You can also use a cookie sheet or large dishpan for the child to dip in if you don't want to use so much bubble soap.

Eggbeater bubbles. Give your child a container of soapy water and an eggbeater with a crank handle to stir up bubbles.

WATER PAINTING AND ART ACTIVITIES

Children enjoy these painting activities. They are allowed to be messy and they can clean up with a garden hose.

Spray-Bottle Painting. Decorate finger paint paper (smooth and glossy) with washable markers. Tape the picture to a shower wall or to the side of the house. Stand back a few feet and spray the picture with a spray bottle filled with water. The colors will blend creating interesting designs.

Paint with Water. Give the children some house paint brushes and buckets of water. Have them pretend to paint the house. They can also paint the sidewalk, the car, and each other.

Mud Painting. Have kids dig up a pile of dirt, and give them a hose to make mud. Allow the children to use old paintbrushes to paint with the mud. They will have just as much fun cleaning it up with the hose.

Rainy-day Art. On a rainy day paint a design of large colorful shapes on paper. Do not let the design dry completely. Set the painting outside in an area where it will get wet. Anchor the corners with rocks to keep the painting from blowing away. After it has been in the rain for a few minutes, bring the painting in and observe the designs, shapes, and splotches created by raindrops.

Body and Sidewalk Painting. Put some nontoxic powdered tempera paints (don't use black— it doesn't wash off well) in containers. Squirt some dish detergent in the containers to help make the paint wash off easier. Then add enough water to make the mixture a thick paint. Don't make it too runny or it will run down the children's arms and legs. Have the children wear swimsuits and let them paint their bodies and the sidewalk. Rinse them off with the hose or sprinkler.

WATER PRETEND ACTIVITIES

Water provides many opportunities for pretend play as children act out daily routines and events.

Car Wash.   Have the child help you wash the car or his or her toy cars. The plastic cars that the children can ride in make good cars to wash.

Wash day.   Set up a laundry center with a clothesline, clothespins, detergent, doll clothes, washboard, and two tubs of water. Let the children use the washboard to wash the doll clothes in the tub. Then they can rinse them out in a tub of clear water. Let them wring out the clothes and hang them to dry.

Washing Dishes. Children love washing dishes. Give them a bucket of warm soapy water and one of clean water. Set out a small dish drainer and some sponges. Give them their pretend dishes and let them wash and dry them.

Fishing. A favorite with kids is pretend fishing. You can play it in a bucket or a kiddie pool. You can make your own lines and fish, but it is easier to get an inexpensive fishing game from the dollar store. These usually use magnets to "catch" the fish.

Fire Fighting. With colored chalk, draw a pretend fire on the side of your house or garage. Use water-filled squirt bottles to put the fire out. As your child squirts, the fire will disappear.

SOCIAL WATER GAMES

Water Balloons. Playing with water balloons is tremendous fun. Buy the small balloons made specifically for water balloons. These balloons make small "bombs" that little kids can handle. Stage a water balloon fight in your yard. This activity makes a spectacular mess in your yard, but kids just love it. Fill a bunch of small water balloons and put them into a cooler or plastic box. Let the kids grab them and throw them at each other. When the balloons are all broken, the game is over. Have a race to see who can pick up the most broken water balloons until they are all picked up. Use a plastic bottle to collect them in: the spout is large enough to put the balloons through, but too small for little hands to reach in and take the balloons out.

Water-Balloon Toss. Another fun water balloon activity is a water balloon toss. Players form two lines facing each other about 6 feet apart. Players in line 1 each toss a water balloon to the opposite players in line 2. Any players who have a balloon burst are out. After each toss, both lines take one step backward and toss again. Repeat until only one pair of players remains. If you don't have a lot of players, don't put anyone out; just keep backing apart the lines until the balloons break at every toss.

Slippery Slides. Spread out long pieces of plastic on the lawn, overlapping the ends. Squirt a little diluted dishwashing soap on the plastic and then wet it down with the hose. Kids love to run and slide on the plastic, especially on a sloped yard. Be sure to invite the neighborhood children to play.

"Duck, Duck, Squirt!" This game is similar to "Duck, Duck, Goose," except instead of saying, "goose," "it" squirts a water gun at a sitting player, who then jumps up and begins the chase.

"Dribble, Dribble, Drench!" This game is another "Duck, Duck, Goose" variation. In this game, "it" goes around the circle with a cup or pitcher of water. When "it" says "dribble" to a player, he or she dribbles a few drops of water on the person's head. When "it" says "drench," he or she dumps the whole cup or pitcher of water on the player's head, starting the chase.

"Marco Polo." This is described in Games (Chapter 7).

Sponge Attack. Collect a bunch of sponges, the larger the better, and, if possible, in a variety of colors. Set out buckets of water on either side of the lawn, or if possible, give a bucket of water to each player. Toss the sponges inside the buckets to get them wet. On the word *Go*, the kids grab a sponge from the bucket and chase each other around the lawn, trying to hit other players with the sponges.

Cold Potato. Using a pin, poke a hole in a water balloon before you fill it with water, so it has a slow but steady leak. Have the players stand in a circle and toss the spraying balloon around from player to player. The person holding the water balloon when it becomes empty is out.

Sponge Tag. In this tag variation, the player who is "it" throws a wet sponge to tag other players.

Water Pistol Fight. This simple game involves the children's running around and shooting each other with water pistols until all are drenched.

WATER PARKS

I confess that I love water parks! I particularly like riding down the huge complex slides on an inner tube, landing with a uncoordinated splash in the receiving pool. My children enjoy them as well. The advantage of water parks over traditional amusement parks is that the lines are much shorter, everyone gets a great deal of exercise, the water keeps everyone cool, and several of the activities are quite relaxing and calming. If your child enjoys water, a water park will be heaven for him or her!

Most water parks have wave pools. These large swimming pools are shallow enough on one end for a child just to wade in and sit in the water. At the other end, the water is usually six to eight feet deep. At the deep end of the pool, there is a wave machine, and every few minutes, the wave machine, will start creating large waves similar to those at the beach. Inner tubes are provided, and people just float in the pool, enjoying the sensation of the waves. After a few minutes of waves, the wave machine stops, and the water is calm for several minutes. Wave pools are generally filled with both adults and children. Smaller, shallow wading pools are also available for small children.

Lazy River rides also provide a soothing and relaxing way to enjoy the water. These are circular streams with a strong current. People float on inner tubes that move with the current.

My child's favorite activity is the water slides. Smaller slides allow the rider to slide down without a tube, but the larger rides require an inner tube to ride. These rides require that you climb up several flights of stairs carrying a tube. The lines are generally fast and short. The line usually splits into two lines at the top, so that you can ride at the same time as your child. The child will probably need assistance several times to get into the tube correctly and wait for the lifeguard's signal to start. I helped my child with this procedure several times waiting for him to start his ride before I got into my tube. I told the lifeguard that my child could not hear well and the lifeguard paid more attention to him, making sure that he waited for the signal to start and was positioned properly in the inner tube.

At the bottom of these rides is a landing pool. The protocol for the rider is to get out of the inner tube and immediately exit from the pool. It took many, many rides before my child would get out of the landing pool without prompting. Again, I told the lifeguard at the bottom that he couldn't hear well and didn't understand, so the lifeguard was able to prompt him to get out of the pool without shouting at him over and over. If you have two adults available, one adult can stay at the bottom of the ride to help. Find a fun, reinforcing water slide and have the child go down it several times.

Other parts to the water park include water play areas with spouts, sprinklers, water fountains, water guns, and waterfalls that the child can stand under and run through. The first time I went to a water park, I was surprised to see adults standing under a huge bucket waiting for it to dump large quantities of water on their heads. My child's fascination with water definitely did not stand out as unusual in this park.

Generally you can change clothes at the water park and store them in a rented locker. Wear your most comfortable swimsuit and swimming shoes. Although you can go barefoot at a water park, it is much more comfortable to have swimming shoes to protect your feet from the hot pavement. Put everything in the locker except the key so you will be free to ride and play in the water with your child. You don't need to carry a towel if the weather is warm enough, and you need to travel light to keep up with the child. If you are taking several children, make sure one adult is assigned to watch your child. It is easy to get lost in large parks. Have your child wear a distinctive swimsuit or a tee shirt so that he or she is easily spotted.

SAND PLAY

Children have always been intrigued by playing in sand. They dig in sand, sift it, build with it, pour it, enjoy the feel and smell of it, pretend with it, and explore how it moves.

Sand, like water, can be a soothing and entertaining medium for young children. Occasionally, even adults can be caught running sand through their fingers, a remnant of the pure stimulatory experiences of childhood.

SAND PLAY MATERIALS
Sand is available at many playgrounds and at the beach. Start collecting your materials into a beach bag or box so that you can carry them with you once you have taught some sand play to your child. We brought our sand toys to the local playground to share with other children. At the beach, we frequently prompted our child to take his sand toys over to other children playing at the beach so he could join them in a cooperative project.

The Sandbox

A sandbox can be made from a children's plastic wading pool or a box with a plastic liner. You can make a small portable sandbox from a large dishpan. Your child should be encouraged to use the sand table or sandbox if there is one available at his or her preschool. The most common type of sand material to use is commercial white play sand which can be found at most home hardware stores and some large toy stores. It is the most hygienic type of sand to use and has the nicest texture. When not in use, the sandbox or table should be covered to keep cats and their associated diseases out.

Sand Play Objects

The list of materials that can be used in sand play is long. Gather up these materials as you find them around the house. Start with just a few items, such as a bucket and a shovel. As your child progresses in sand play, continue to add to the available materials.

- Buckets, bowls and containers
- Mixing bowls and baking bowls, pans, and utensils
- Shovels and scoops
- Spoons of various types and materials
- Spatulas, soup ladles, kitchen equipment
- Measuring cups and spoons
- Colanders and sieves
- Small pitchers
- Plastic paint scrapers
- Small fish nets
- Small flags
- Flat pieces of wood
- Plastic flowers and vases
- Plastic dishes
- Toy furniture and dolls
- Funnels
- Shakers with large holes (i.e., Parmesan cheese shakers)
- Potato mashers
- Shells, rocks, and pebbles of various types
- Gardening tools, watering cans, and gloves
- Small plastic animals, dinosaurs, and figurines
- Cars and trucks, construction equipment including a crane
- Popsicle sticks
- String
- Small twigs, nuts, and pine cones
- Cardboard tubes and Ping-Pong balls
- Berry containers and net bags from onions or fruit
- Feathers
- Jars and lids
- Rubber puzzle pieces
- Toy trains and accessories

- ➤ Corrugated cardboard
- ➤ Rolling pins
- ➤ Craft and play jewels
- ➤ Clothespins
- ➤ Marbles
- ➤ Sand wheels and combs
- ➤ Aquarium gravel
- ➤ Pipes, tubes, cylinders
- ➤ Magnifiers
- ➤ Cloth scraps

SENSORY ACTIVITIES AND EXPLORATORY PLAY

Start teaching play with nonpurposeful play. Show your child how to explore and manipulate the sand and sand toys by pouring, scooping, sifting, digging, smoothing, rubbing, combing, patting, and packing the sand. Bring out all the sand tools and materials and show him or her things to do with them. Explore the texture of the sand with combs and wheels. Pack sand in containers and dump them out. Pour sand from container to container. Pour water into the sand. Explore the texture and changes in the sand from the addition of water. Use different scoops and spoons to dig in the sand. These early unstructured activities let the child explore the qualities of sand, expanding what might be his or her very limited interaction with the material.

Allow ample time for these experiences of nonstructured sand play. The adult must monitor the child carefully during unstructured sand play for inappropriate behavior. If your child finds sand play reinforcing, then you can insist that he or she play with it appropriately. Teach the child that he or she will be removed from the sand activity if he or she persists in playing with the sand inappropriately (for example, eating it or rubbing it on the face). To utilize the child's interest in sand, allow him or her to engage *briefly* in an appropriate activity that the child finds reinforcing (running it through the fingers), and then have the child perform a different appropriate task (pouring the sand from cup to cup). In this way, you are not allowing any extremely inappropriate play (eating sand or throwing it), nor are you allowing the child to perseverate on an appropriate activity (running the sand through the fingers). If sand is a major stimulation for your child, this process may allow you to introduce new targets by interrupting the child's stimulatory behavior. This process might take some time and can be difficult, but your goal is to teach the child that he or she can have fun with sand in other ways besides just running it through the fingers or staring at it.

Once the child can manipulate the sand by pouring, packing, combing, and scooping begin to introduce more purposeful play. Digging in sand is fun. Using different tools, dig holes of various sizes and depth. Pour water into the holes and observe what happens. Dig lines, shapes, letters, paths and "roads." Use rakes, shovels, spoons, scoops, sticks, fingers, toes, and cups to make your holes and paths. Put the sand in pails as you dig, and then dump it out in a big pile. Sand and water make a great combination of play materials. In your sandbox, pour water from different containers into and onto the sand, making pools, moats, and rivers. At the beach, you can explore the changes that waves and tidal pools make on the sand. Have the child make mud pies and squish the wet sand with fingers and feet.

SAND PRETEND ACTIVITIES

Sand is a wonderful and versatile medium to use for pretend activities. Try some of these activities with your child in his or her sandbox or at the beach.

Make a Pond. Dig a big hole in the sandbox and fill it with water. Pretend it is a pond with little fish. "Feed" the fish with sand. Be a frog and catch flies with your tongue. Go "fishing."

Make a Garden. Have the child dress up as a farmer. Using children's or small adult garden tools, create a garden in the sandbox. Rake the sand and make rows. Dig holes, plant seeds in the holes, and use a watering can to water the plants.

Be Snakes in the Desert. Wiggle on your belly in the sand!

Go to the Beach. Play with the sand toys, run to the ocean, sit in a beach chair, and hunt for shells in the sand. Put up an umbrella and sit in the shade.

Pirates! Use a pirate ship and figurines. Set up the scenes and arrange the figurines. Have them sail the ship, sword fight, swim in the ocean, and look for treasure.

Dress up Like Pirates. Dig for buried treasure! Bury some coins and craft jewels in the sand and hunt for them, or bury a small box with the treasure in it.

Be a Dog. Dig like a dog and bury a "bone."

Create Animal Scenes. Get out all your animal figurines and create scenes from the ocean, jungle, or desert. Make some hills and water holes and arrange the animals talking about them and moving them in short scenes.

Food. Make pretend food. Have a tea party or a meal. Pretend to cook using sand and kitchen containers.

SAND BUILDING

Building with sand is very popular at the beach. Teach your child to make mounds, hills, sandcastle towers, and sea monsters.

Sand Forms. Pack damp sand into various containers and turn them over to make mounds and shapes.

Sand Prints. Use plastic molds or any sort of object to make prints in smoothed sand. Make handprints and footprints. Make "animal prints" using different materials.

Sand-Castle Building. The commercial molds that are designed for building sand castles are not very effective. To build solid sandcastles or other buildings, you need water to mix with the sand. Water is the glue that holds the sand together, so you need to have plenty available from a garden hose or a big bucket of water. Mix the sand and water in a bucket and make sure the sand is very wet. If you are at the beach, you can dig with a shovel down to the water table to get to the wet sand. To start making a sandcastle tower, scoop out a big, double handful of very wet sand from the bottom of the hole or bucket. Make a base mound with this double handful. Then start building your castle on top of this mound. Put a handful of wet sand on the mound and flatten it into a pancake by gentle jiggling. What you are trying to do is to distribute the water in the wet sand so that each pancake will bind to the sand below. To make a tower, stack pancakes on top of each other and use the same maneuver to glue each pancake to the one below. As you build the tower, use progressively smaller handfuls so that the tower tapers at the top and doesn't get top-heavy and fall over. Once your tower is built, you can try carving into the side of the castle to make designs and turrets. To make walls that can connect the towers together, grab a double handful of wet sand from your bucket. Hold the sand between your hands and jiggle it so that the sand takes on a brick shape. Lay a series of bricks end to end to make the bottom layer of the wall. Continue to add layers on top of the bottom layer of the wall until it is high enough.

Sea Monster. Building a big sea monster is easily done at the beach. Let the child start making a long mound of sand while you dig around it to accentuate the height of the creation. Shape the sand into fins coming out from the side and back. Carve a mouth and use shells for teeth.

Construction Site. Get out all your trucks, dump trucks, cranes, cars, and other props you can find and make a big construction site. Make sand buildings and knock them down. Load the dump truck with sand and dump it. Move objects with the crane. Build roads and move your vehicles along them.

Roads. Make roads for your miniature cars. Make hills and use empty cans (tops and bottoms cut off) for tunnels. Race your cars and crash them.

SAND ART

Sand art activities are messy so try to do them outside. To make a sand picture, use a squirt bottle of glue to paint a picture on cardboard. Then put sand on the wet glue and shake off the excess to form a picture. At first, use just one color and keep the picture simple (the child's name or a shape). Later you can do this in stages. First draw part of the picture and put colored sand on it. Let it dry. Then paint another part of the picture and use another color of sand. Some commercial sand art products use sticky paper so that you can peel off the covers to each part of the picture one at a time using different colored sand to form a picture. These work pretty well but should probably be reserved for older children. Another sand activity involves pouring colored sand into a glass container to create layers of sand. Some commercial kits are available to make these sand scenes.

SENSORY BOX

Other materials can provide some of the same exploratory play activities as sand. For example, fill a box with rice, beans, or macaroni. Have the child explore the materials with his or her hands or use a scoop to pour the materials from container to container. Have the child look for "treasure" and surprises in the box. These sensory boxes seem to be an occupational therapy favorite.

Chapter 11
Arts and Crafts

- *The Craft Box*
- *General Suggestions*
- *Craft Ideas*
- *Craft Recipes*
- *Craft Resources*

Helping your child create craft projects can develop his or her creativity, fine motor skills, and a sense of pride in accomplishment. Making crafts with a playdate can be a fun and relaxed way for the child to experience peer play. The best craft projects create usable finished products that the child can play with and pretend with. Early experiences with arts and crafts should concentrate on easy to manipulate materials and short projects so that the child does not get frustrated. The short attention spans and limited fine motor skills of preschool children make it more important for the teaching adult to emphasize the process and fun of the experience rather than the final product. Teach the children to be successful in creating crafts by making the projects short and simple. Teach also that there is no right or wrong way to be creative. When working with the child, help him or her understand what is going on by naming each object, tool or material you are working with and talking about what you are doing. Do the crafts with the child by demonstrating the uses of the different materials and creating your own object.

When creating art and craft projects with young children, do not let your own ego become entwined with the child's finished product. Do not be concerned if the finished product is messy, distorted, or simply not "cute." For many adults, it takes a lot of self-control and self-confidence to simply let children do their own thing. If you are tempted to do all the cutting and pasting for the child so a project turns out "right," stop and ask yourself: "What am I teaching?"

THE CRAFT BOX

To be prepared at all times for the creation of crafts, keep a big box or boxes of supplies to use in arts and crafts activities. As you become more experienced in creating crafts with your children, you will be able to think of a project with the materials that you have on hand. It's nice to be prepared for rainy days and last minute playdates. Supplies that I keep on hand include:

- Craft glue, glue pens and tubes, fabric glue, and other types of glue
- A variety of paints (finger, tempera, water, powered, tubed, glow-in-the-dark)
- Paint brushes, sponges, and rubber stamps
- Construction paper, heavy watercolor or other heavy painting paper, butcher block paper, tissue paper, Crayons, various markers, colored pencils, sidewalk chalk and other chalks

➢ Scissors (type depending on safety level of kids)
➢ Old wallpaper and wrapping paper
➢ Glitter, sequins, and craft jewels
➢ Ribbons, felt, fabric scraps, and buttons
➢ Shaving cream
➢ Cardboard items (toilet paper rolls, paper towel rolls, oatmeal cylinders, shoe boxes)
➢ Stickers of all varieties and stars
➢ Yarn and string
➢ Cotton balls
➢ Q tips (for applying glue)
➢ Toothpicks
➢ Cupcake liners, coffee filters
➢ Magazines
➢ Small plastic containers (clean Jello, yogurt, and margarine cups)
➢ Seasonal supplies from around the yard such as flower petals, acorns, leaves, etc.
➢ Iron-on Velcro strips
➢ Noodles and pasta shapes (elbow, bow tie, rigatoni, spaghetti, shells, etc.)
➢ Cereal (Cheerios, Alphabits, Fruit Loops, etc.)
➢ Dried beans, seeds, nuts, rice

I don't keep the food items in the box, but everything else is kept together in a cabinet dedicated to art and craft supplies. Keeping a cabinet supplied with this kind of stuff has provided a lot of fun over the years in our house. When in a pinch, you can just pull it out and have the children do just about any sort of craft project you can think of.

We did not spend too much time on crafts in our home program because my son went to preschool where craft projects were done every day. I think if your child can handle preschool, the artwork and socialization done there can be very helpful in developing your child's arts and crafts playskills. During playdates, we did do several simple craft projects that were generally successful.

GENERAL SUGGESTIONS FOR ARTS AND CRAFTS PROJECTS

➢ Keep all art projects *short*.
➢ Try some seasonal or holiday-related projects (snowmen, valentines, etc.).
➢ Make an engaging activity out of collecting materials for crafts. For example, take a nature walk to collect things, and then make a collage.
➢ Plan for the art skills of all involved children.
➢ Concentrate on the fun of the process, not the completed product.
➢ Do any piercing, stapling, ironing, and heating yourself.
➢ Carefully supervise cutting and gluing.
➢ Cover the work areas with old newspapers, old sheets, or old shower curtains.

CRAFT IDEAS

Decorating Shapes and Objects

Kids love to decorate anything. So before you start teaching them how to create complex projects, consider having them decorate preshaped or preformed items of different materials. This is a much easier activity than trying to draw something or construct something. The finished product is always recognizable, and it has your child's personal touch. Shapes cut out from watercolor paper, dried clay creations, and little unpainted wooden objects can all be decorated. Have the children decorate the items with paint, fabric glue, sequins, stickers, and other items from your craft supplies. Older children can draw or paint designs on the shape or object.

Decorating Dress-up Items and T-shirts.

Children love to wear their creations. We decorated felt dress-up items and plain T-shirts on several occasions. My son still uses his pirate vest and crown that he made in playdates. I made up the red felt vests for all the children using a simple pattern that I drew on a piece of paper. I had a friend sew up the sides. The children decorated the vests using fabric paint, glue, sequins, glitter, and little craft jewels. The crowns were made from yellow felt, and I ironed on Velcro for a closure. I like to save this activity for the end of the playdate so that the kids are seated and calm. The glue and fabric paint take overnight to dry, so you can give the finished project to the playdate's mother for safekeeping until the morning. You can also use plain white T-shirts for decoration or any other sort of dress-up item you might create such as hats and belts.

Brush Painting

Painting is always fun. To make it more entertaining for your child, cut out shapes from heavy paper prior to the playdate or project. Watercolor paper is good for these shapes. Let each child decorate or paint the shape using whatever craft materials you have at hand. This process creates a recognizable object regardless of your child's art skills. At a craft store, you can also buy little wooden shapes to paint and decorate. Another painting idea involves hanging a large sheet of mural or butcher block paper. Before a playdate, draw a simple scene. For example, draw a beach and ocean. During the playdate, have the children paint fish and shells on the scene, or you can have the children decorate ocean-related shapes and tape them on the mural.

Finger Painting

Some children love the sensory feel of finger painting. Try using different types of finger paint on different materials. Finger painting is a good activity to do outside in the summer so the children can wash off easily with the hose. Try letting the children roll marbles on the paint or combine finger painting with sponge painting. Shaving cream finger painting is always a big hit with kids. Use shaving cream mounds with a little tempera paint poured on top and let the kids finger-paint with the mixture.

Collages

Collages are great fun for children. There aren't any rules and nothing ever looks the same twice. You can do color collages, shapes collages, magazine picture collages, texture collages, and nature collages. Have the children gather the items that they want to use and let them attach the items to the collage backing.

Puppets

Puppets can be made from a variety of materials. You can create sock puppets, cut-out puppets attached to a popsicle stick, and lunch sack puppets. Alien puppets can be made with soft gloves (the fingers are the arms and legs of the alien). Paper finger puppets can be made from stiff paper. Cut two holes in the bottom of the paper. The children stick their first two fingers through to make the "legs" of the puppet. Encourage the children to play with the puppets after they create them.

CRAFT RECIPES

Plenty of nontoxic commercial paints are available for both brush and finger painting. For a few other specialty paints, try these ideas.

Puff Paint

This paint will puff up when dry, giving an unusual texture to a painting.
1 c. flour
1 c. salt
1 c. water
Tempera paint
Plastic squeeze bottle

In a small mixing bowl, stir together flour, salt, and water. Add several teaspoons of tempera paint. Stir. Pour into a plastic squeeze bottle. On a covered work surface, squeeze paint onto paper. Sprinkle glitter on the paint while it is still wet to add some sparkle. Do not use the paint on fabric.

Plastic Starch Finger Paint

Spread liquid starch over dry paper. Sprinkle powder tempera paint onto the liquid starch. The children will have fun using their hands to mix the powdered paint with the starch. You may add liquid dish washing soap to the mixture to make clean up easier.

Clown Paint

1/8 c. baby lotion
1/4 tsp. powdered tempera paint
1 squirt liquid dish washing soap
Mix the ingredients to make a paint that is easily removed with soap and water. This mixture can be used for face paint. Be sure to test the skin first for any possible reactions to the ingredients.

Sparkle Paints

This paint mixture contains salt, which makes the paint sparkle when dry.
Mix equal parts of flour, water, and salt. Pour some of the mixture into squeeze bottles. Add tempera paint to each bottle and shake well. Squeeze or brush the paint onto paper, creating a design, word, or picture.

CRAFT RESOURCES

Preschool Teachers

Preschool teachers are great sources for arts and crafts projects. If your child goes to preschool and comes home with something that looks good and your child seemed to enjoy the activity, save the project and reproduce it in your playgroups and playdates. You can also ask the teacher where he or she gets her ideas.

The World Wide Web

I think the best source for craft ideas is the WWW (World Wide Web). Numerous birthday party theme sites and craft sites for children have simple activities and projects. These are usually free and some have printable instructions and cutouts. A few minutes searching on one of these sites can give you plenty of ideas, but remember, the tried and true simple activities (decorating objects and painting, for example) are frequently the best! The WWW party theme and craft sites that I like are listed below by their names (you will have to do a search on your search engine to get the exact URL):

➢ KinderArt
➢ Michael's
➢ Kinderplanet Crafts
➢ Makestuff.com
➢ Hands on Crafts for Kids
➢ Makingfriends.com
➢ The Mining Company Crafts for Kids
➢ Arts and Craft Projects for Preschoolers
➢ Camp Crafts
➢ Crayola.com
➢ The Mailbox
➢ GuideZone Crafts
➢ Hobby Lobby Project Sheets
➢ Jim Speirs' Scouting Page
➢ Squigly's Arts & Crafts for Kids
➢ DLTK's Printable Crafts for Kids
➢ Bizarre Stuff You can Make in Your Kitchen
➢ KinderCrafts - Enchanted Learning Software
➢ Danielle's Place
➢ Eileen's Camp Crafts and Other Fun Things
➢ Berit's Best Sites for Children
➢ Fun For Kids by Jen
➢ Home Arts: Rainy Day Projects
➢ Kids Domain Crafts
➢ GusTown: Craft Corner

Chapter 12
Playdates

- *Early Peer Interactions*
- *Playdates Versus Playgroups*
- *Playdate Goals*
- *Playdate Prerequisites*
- *Playdate Peers*
- *The Playdate Peer Pool*
- *Types of Peers*
- *Peer Preparation*
- *Playdate Structure*
- *Early Playdates*
- *Evolving Playdates*
- *The Theme Structure*
- *The Preschool Structure*
- *Unstructured Playdates*

EARLY PEER INTERACTIONS

Exposing your child to other people and public places early on is important. Before your child is ready for formal playdates, have your child be around other kids as much as possible. Even if your child can't participate in any group activities or doesn't have many independent play skills, just hanging out with the other kids is helpful. Have your child practice tolerating proximity to people and peers. This practice might be painful for you as a result of your child's behaviors, but try to develop a skin of steel and take your child out in public as much as possible.

A playground, with all its noise and confusion, can be highly disorienting to our children. To develop tolerance for the playground, your child should visit it often over a long period of time. Your child can practice early play skills (these may involve just tolerating other children nearby) while you are pushing the child on the swing at the park or while he or she is climbing on the equipment.

One idea is to go to McDonald's and use their small on-site playground. If your child likes to climb and play on the equipment, then this place provides a great opportunity for the child just to be around other kids without the burden of interacting. Also if you go at off-peak times, likely only one or two other children will be there. This type of activity that involves large motor movement with minimal child-child interaction is much less stressful and "hothouse-like" than trying to get your child to play with toys indoors with another child. This type of informal activity can be used frequently over a long period of time while you are working on more sophisticated playskills and arranging more formal playdates.

Another idea is to bring toys to share at a public playground or pool. My child fixated on sand, water, mud, and dirt. So we brought beach toys to the local playground, which had a sandy base and allowed my child to play appropriately in the sand. The other kids flocked to our little beach setup—they were somewhat younger than my son, who was 5 (they were 3 and 4), but he was able to play with the toys and sand while they were using his toys too. He didn't have to interact with the children too much, except on occasion to ask for toys. There is considerably less pressure in this situation than in a one-on-one playdate where an aide is standing over the child counting interactions. Once we brought his pirate ship to the pool and even kids older than my son came over to play with it. In the summer, bring your coolest toys out into the front yard and start playing with them. My son had a large electric Jeep that was wildly popular with the neighborhood boys. They were not allowed to play with it, however, unless they included my son in their play. My son's "slip and slide" and his Jeep made my son reinforcing to the peers and they were therefore more likely to interact with him.

These informal ideas, of course, expose your child to public places and all sorts of people, including peers, without placing many demands. They allow him or her to be in a parallel play situation playing activities that he or she knows well without having to interact with other children other than to share toys.

PLAYDATES VERSUS PLAYGROUPS

Formal activities that teach peer playskills include both *playdates* (one or two peers) and *playgroups* (several peers). These two activities differ and they teach different things. To plan which type of play interaction to use, you need to think carefully about what specific playskills the child needs to be taught.

Playdates can be harder for the child because he or she has to concentrate the whole time on one child and use language to communicate with his or her friend. The activities also tend to be more intense. In contrast, a playgroup situation offers more opportunity for your child just to hang out or play in a parallel manner. In playgroups, a child can also learn to follow along with the group without a lot of language. However, in playgroups, the child might not get as intense socialization and language practice as in a one-on-one playdate. Peers in playgroups may not interact as much with your child, and they may even reject your child unless they have had proper preparation. In addition, playgroups are much harder to organize than playdates and ultimately may take up more time from and effort by the planning adult than they are worth in teaching playskills to your child.

In planning your playdates and playgroups, try to avoid what I call the "birthday party" trap. Don't overdo it! Often in planning playdates and playgroups, the mom gets so overworked in making sure the kid or kids are involved in activities for every second of the playdate or playgroup that she ends up entertaining the children and wearing herself out. This trap is particularly true in playgroups. With only one peer, you can be fairly informal ("Hey, let's play catch"), but you have to have more crowd control and structure with a playgroup.

To avoid this trap, see if the children can just hang together and pretend in a pretend center or in occasional unstructured activities rather than guiding them through thirty exhausting theme based activities. On playdates, try some low-key activities, and then reward the children with a trip to the dollar store or ice cream shop. Believe me, the peer will remember that last part more than any sort of tantrum or other unpleasantness during the playdate.

PLAYDATE GOALS

Structured and formal playdates and playgroups are important for several reasons. They can provide intense and repetitive practice with playskills and socialization in a controlled environment. They can create a means for establishing friendships in childhood. In a playdate or playgroup, the child can generalize what he or she has learned in therapy and practice observational learning in a small group. The child can also get used to being around peers and children rather than constantly interacting only with adults. The ultimate goal is for the child to find it more reinforcing to be with friends than with his or her tutors.

Playdates need to be run and managed by a trained person who is capable of instructional control over both the children. A tutor should always be present to assist the peer and the child in interacting with each other. The tutors or parents need to be highly energetic, fun, creative, and willing to get silly and dirty. They must also be keenly aware of the child's skills and language abilities. It is important to know what each child likes. Play is a personal thing, and not all children like all activities. You really need to know what your child likes to do and "mine" that interest. Don't drag out finger paints in a playdate if your child can't stand to get his or her hands dirty (work on that sensory issue elsewhere). Playdates need to be reinforcing to both the child and the peer.

How you set goals and take data depends on your consultant and method of therapy. I do believe that you should set some goals to give you guidance on what you are teaching. The problem is that play, by its very nature, is not goal-oriented, and it is a delicate balance to teach play without making it tedious or aversive. In addition, as the child progresses through playdates, the playdate structure must become less and less rigid, so that spontaneous, self-reinforcing play can begin to take over. If you monitor your child's initial playdate experiences by standing over the child, counting interactions with a golf counter, you will need to think carefully how you are going to reduce that structure at some point and yet still keep your goals in mind.

I think goals are important for all the tutors to keep in mind, but tutors must be able to switch gears and focus on something not on the goal list if it appears spontaneously in play. Any sort of independent interaction with a peer or creative thinking needs to be heavily reinforced. The tutor or adult must also be willing to let the children just hang out at times. If they choose to watch a video and they are sitting together holding hands and giggling while watching, then that non-verbal closeness and shared experience should be allowed to continue even if the board game has been left unfinished. As the peer gains confidence, the adult should try to fade his or her presence—starting off by using a good cover like "I'm going to get something to drink."

Goal setting can be facilitated by spending time just observing your child play both with and without a peer. It is critical for you to observe both your child at free play (if he or she does any) and also the peer. Be aware of normal play interactions and duration. Goals can be set based on those observations. Do not impose an adult concept of play on the children. There is little point in setting a goal of 15 minutes of game interaction with a peer if the child cannot sustain any sort of activity for that duration even with an adult. Keep developmental appropriateness in mind. Small children have *very* short attention spans normally and like repetition. If you are using older peers, remember that they are going to have longer attention spans than even a typical child of the same age as your child. Keep everything simple and short.

Sample goals you might work on and document might include duration of unprompted participation, independent responses to peers, independent initiations with peers, independent turn-taking, and spontaneous observational learning. You should try to develop some intermediate goals that allow for improvement and flexibility, such as increased eye contact, proximity to the peer, and duration of appropriate parallel play.

Recall that the normal development of social play with peers evolves from parallel play, which includes tolerating a peer, observing a peer, and imitating a peer, to progressively more reciprocal and cooperative play. Try to keep that development in mind so that you can see when progress is being made.

We have a behavioral checklist that we complete after each playdate. The checklist includes: participates in play activities, follows group and conditional directions, remains with peer(s), initiates verbal interaction or play, responds to peer conversation, and refrains from stereotypic behavior (we got most of these from A Work In Progress*). More specifically our playdate goals are these:*
Social conversation — *initiating a conversation with a peer, responding to peer statements, maintaining conversation with peer for 3 turns;*
Imaginative play with a peer — *initiating an imaginative play activity with a peer, following peer lead in an imaginative play activity (it is so hard for her to follow another's imagination);*
Behavior — *Remaining with an activity until completion (also hard); no scripting during the playdate; following group, conditional, and novel directions.*

PLAYDATE PREREQUISITES

Your child needs to have some playskills before embarking on playdates. He or she should be able to tolerate being around other children. In therapy with a tutor, the child should be able to handle some toys correctly, work some with manipulatives, play with sensory materials (playdough, sand, and water), know a social game or two, sing and/or act out some songs, and perhaps be able to play a simple game. The child should be able to do some activities outside such as play on playground equipment or in a wading or regular pool.

The ability to dress up and pretend in a pretend play center is also very helpful. Some advanced skills include the ability to participate in circle-time activities, listen to short stories, and use art skills. However, keep in mind your own play as a child. Did *you* consider circle time to be play? I doubt it. So be careful about introducing school skills into a playdate and calling it play (teach them somewhere else).

The use of playstations in therapy can teach the child to move from activity to activity without transition issues and can also teach the child to follow someone when he or she is playing. Each playstation is a different activity, for example a manipulative or a pretend play center. You can set up a few playstations in therapy and practice moving from one activity to the next with the child. Practice having the child follow you from playstation to playstation, using verbal prompts that are age-appropriate ("Hey, let's play house now"). As this activity progresses, have the child lead you from one activity to another. Finally, the tutor and child can alternate taking the lead.

The most important prerequisite skill for playdates is *language*. Make sure that your main therapy is working hard on some form of communication for your child. At the very least, your child should have a method of making his or her desires and requests known. In some way, he or she should be able to ask for things from both adults and peers. The more language your child has, the easier it will be for him or her to interact with the peer. In retrospect, I wish we had spent a whole lot more time on language in our home Applied Behavioral Analysis (ABA) therapy and less time teaching my child to play with a huge number of toys and arranging playdates and playgroups.

PLAYDATE PEERS

It is important to spend some time finding the right playdate peers for your child. This is an arduous and ongoing process. Early highly structured one-on-one playdate peers should be probably be 5 years old or older as they have the maturity to take direction and lead your child. However, same age or younger children can also be helpful for more unstructured playdates and in playgroup play because they might be closer to the same developmental level as your child and won't place as many demands on him or her. Children in playgroups can be both younger and older than your child. The peers should be upbeat, energetic, and attentive. Try to find kids with decent manners. Patience and understanding are also helpful but sometimes have to be nurtured in the peers through preparation and reminders. Look for children who are good models. They should have reasonably good group skills, take direction, willingly participate in a variety of activities, and be tolerant toward other children.

Unfortunately, you will find that other people's kids can have the most horrendous manners. You want to avoid those unmannerly children if possible, but you probably will still find yourself in the role of disciplining other kids. This need occurs especially in playgroup situations with several children, as instructional control tends to deteriorate rapidly. Fortunately, it is easy to use your behavioral knowledge with typical kids. They will literally blossom before your eyes with tons of positive reinforcement, clear, specific instructions, and consistent consequences and follow-through. Many children are so used to listening to lectures and sophisticated language from their parents (which they have learned to ignore) that they can be shocked (and actually relieved) to meet a adult of action, not words.

My neighbor's typical sons like to play with PlayDoh, put together puzzles, cut, color, glue, paint, draw with sidewalk chalk, read books, and play with Legos. My children do these types of activities here at home too. But when there is a group of kids, these activities take a back seat to the run, chase, and scream type of play. In order to do structured types of activities with my neighbor's boys here, it takes tons of adult supervision—or the scissors will end up as dinosaurs trying to eat other people. PlayDoh would get thrown. The one quiet interactive type of activity that they will all play together is with Thomas the Tank Engine toys. The only time things get loud is when they fight over a piece.

THE PLAYDATE POOL

The purpose of a playdate pool is to provide different types of peers for your child and to avoid burnout. Try to create a pool of children of both sexes and a range of ages. Try to schedule regular playdate times each week, and vary your peers from week to week. A peer might burn out if he or she participates in more than one or two playdates a week over a long period of time.

If your child goes to preschool with a shadow aide, have the shadow aide scope out the kids and approach the other moms with offers to have their child play with your child. Usually, the other parents will be able to check out your child at open houses, school carnivals, and so forth. Their child can also fill them in on your child's behavior and reassure them. The shadow aide can prepare the peer at school prior to the playdate. If the playdate is fun and reinforcing to the peer, the peer will tell the other kids at school, and your pool may expand as the other kids want to get in on the fun.

Siblings can be used as playdate peers, but frequently these children require some special handling. My older son had a hard time providing peer therapy and playdates because he is a sensitive, highly creative child, and it was hard for him to play at our ASD child's level. He also was smaller than our ASD child although he was two years older, and this difference in size made any kind of physical play difficult. Now that both of my sons are older, they are able to play together more as brothers. Remember that siblings (especially if there is only one) have to live with and deal with the ASD child daily and may have experienced a lot of unpleasantness over the years. The sibling also has to deal with jealousy over his or her perception (perhaps true) that the ASD child gets excessive attention. If the sibling is willing and interested in playdates, then by all means, use him or her. Otherwise I would not press the issue. As the sibling grows older and more mature, he or her may be able to be more involved in playdates.

My son (age nine) enjoys playing with action figures with his three-and-a-half-year-old brother, who has fairly advanced play skills and language. Both have vivid imaginations, and it's fun to hear them talk about what their "men" are doing.

Neighborhood children may also seem like a good playdates, but in our case it was not until my older child made good friends with some of them that they would play with our child and then only on an informal basis. When I approached the parents, I was stonewalled (politely, of course). In our case, the neighborhood children had had some unpleasant experiences with our child and avoided him until they were able to understand the situation.

Other possible places to find peers include the children of friends (although I was surprised at the reluctance of some—I really didn't get any peers in this way). Neighborhood and athletic organizations might provide some kids. Our best source of playdate peers was preschool. At school try to have the shadow pick out a child that will stay with your child at recess or play center time and then come home with him or her for a playdate.

Another option is the siblings of children that go to your various therapists. For example, the siblings of children who use your speech-language pathologist or occupational therapist. The parents are usually very understanding, and the siblings are accustomed to special needs behavior. In addition, sometimes it is easier for them to deal with your child than with their own siblings.

Perhaps I would have had greater success in talking to parents to recruit peers if I had not focused on my child's underlying need for playdates or a playgroup. Instead, it is probably better to focus on the activities that the other parents' children are going to be doing and how much fun it is going to be for *their* child. If the parents don't know your child, use some vague and generic description of his problem (i.e., language delay) rather than going into a lot of detail (believe me, this generalizing will save you a lot of grief and many lengthy conversations).

In any event, parents are mostly interested in their own children's development, so focus on what their child will get from the experience rather than on your child. In addition to the fun of the activities, point out how teaching their child to help another child play can improve confidence, develop empathy, and strengthen tolerance. Finally, remember that most parents are happy to take advantage of a few hours of regular, organized, safe, and fun childcare.

Look for parents who are somewhat relaxed about their child, or you will end up spending a lot of time reassuring them. Parents with several older children tend to be more relaxed about their younger children and will welcome a break. Avoid peers whose parents are super overprotective or strictly politically correct and won't let their child play anything they deem violent (Pokemon, Star Wars, cowboys, Power Rangers, sword fights) or sexist (Barbie Dolls, Princess dress-up, play makeup).

One child became very distraught when we pulled out a Dr. Seuss book because his parents forbade Dr. Seuss in their home. Who knew? I never thought to ask other parents if there was something that we would NOT be allowed to do. I assumed that "gun play" was not a safe bet. It just never occurred to me that other very traditional activities and play would not be considered appropriate.

TYPES OF PEERS

There are as many different kinds of peers as there are types of children. When choosing peers, try to find a variety of children with different types of skills and preferences. Some of the types of peers you will encounter include:

The Teacher. This peer can be overbearing but is helpful because he or she can give instructions to the child. In peer-play situations that are highly structured and more similar to therapy, this type of peer can be very helpful in applying playskill learned in therapy to actual play. On the other hand, be careful not to let the peer get too tutor-like—learning to play with a peer should not be exactly like playing with an adult.

The Athlete. This peer is good for physical activities and games like ball play, tag, Nintendo, wrestling, bike riding, skating, and climbing.

The Actor. This peer is wonderful for acting out plays, dress-up, and pretending.

The Conversationalist. This peer is helpful for teaching conversational patterns to the child. This peer is also good for watching or listening to stories and commenting.

The Listener. This peer is quiet and somewhat passive. He or she may allow your child to practice in quiet activities such as story time and watching videos. He or she can provide a model for quiet sitting and paying attention.

The Big Brother. Children with younger siblings are comfortable with children who have limited language and have developed ways to play with their little siblings that they can transfer into a playdate. Siblings of special needs children can be very good at this and may enjoy working with a special needs child who is not their sibling.

PEER PREPARATION

Preparing the peers is helpful. Because they are so young, they are not likely to be able to initiate and sustain interaction with your child without some assistance and training. This inability is especially true if your child is a nonresponder, that is, if he or she tends to ignore a verbal or other type of initiation from a peer or tends to walk away. The peers might also be discouraged by your child's unusual or inappropriate behaviors. You need to warn the peers about these behaviors and give them tools to deal with them. If they are schoolmates, this nonresponsiveness is usually less an issue as they are used to your child already.

You may want to meet with the peer separately to discuss the playdate. Some parents have written a little training manual and reviewed it with the peer prior to the playdate. Others have just talked to the peer informally and demonstrated examples of behaviors the peer might encounter in the playdate. These behaviors and suggested responses may be role-played with the peer prior to the playdate. Points to cover in this briefing include telling the peer about any unusual behaviors your child has and how to deal with them or when to ignore them. The briefing should also include training the peer to initiate and sustain interactions. Children are often shy about reprimanding or pushing themselves on another child. Teach the peer to use language like "Hey, stop that," or "Stop grabbing!" Also teach the peer to get your child's attention: "Hey child, I'm talking to you" as they tap the child on the shoulder or touch his or her arm. The peer should be given follow-up language if the initial attempt doesn't work: "HEY CHILD! Catch this ball!"

The peer should also be taught to respond to atypical efforts of your child to initiate an interaction, that is, your child's just shoving a toy in his or her face or pulling the peer by the hand to an activity. It is extremely important that the peer be taught to recognize such an atypical social initiation and respond to it appropriately. You do not want your child to experience social rejection in early playdates. Later, you can help your child recognize and deal with the social rejection that he or she might experience in playgroups and informal settings, but for now you want your child to learn appropriate initiations and interactions in a nonthreatening and reinforcing situation. Appropriate peer response to a child's social initiation reinforces that child's social initiation behavior. The child will then be encouraged to continue to initiate socially. Until the child's play and social skills are stronger, he or she should not be discouraged from initiating an interaction by a nonresponse or outright rejection from a peer.

During a playgroup, if my child didn't respond to a peer the first time, a tutor would have been whispering in his ear, prompting him to respond. However, when a peer fails to respond to my son, it seems to be my son's problem and not the peer's problem. My son must have done something wrong. He must not have demonstrated appropriate nonverbal gestures. I watched a peer not respond to my son during a playgroup session and I thought the whole scene looked ridiculous. We prompted our son to ask "Johnny" to play tic tac toe on the driveway since two other kids were engaged in it and our son was watching. He walked up to Johnny and said, "Hey! Lets play tic tac toe." (Johnny was just standing there.) Johnny turned and started walking away to other toys. My tutors then prompted our kid to get his attention. Our son ran after him tapping him on the shoulder and saying "Hey! Let's play!" Johnny finally gave some sort of communicative gesture in the form of a shrug. My tutor then ran over to get our son to stop him from trying to interact. Our son was literally confused. Here he was pushed and pushed to get this kid to play, then he was rejected, and then the tutors tell him to leave the kid alone. No wonder he got weepy and cried out, "Johnny won't play with me!"

During the briefing, also set up a prompt system for the peer, so that the adult can stay on the periphery of play and prompt the peer by using hand signals or flash cards. For a while, you will not be able to stay in the background. For several playdates, you might have to be right on top of the kids, but as the playdates progress, a prompt system will provide a mechanism for fading yourself out. For example, you might set up a signal prompt to the peer to get the child's attention or to respond to an atypical initiation from the child. The peer can be given signals to use to leave the playdate, to take a break, and to ask for adult assistance.

The advantage of a signal system is that it allows the adult to avoid using excessive language to prompt the peer. Too much verbal prompting by the adult is distracting to both children and interferes with the flow of play. You will be trying to support interactive play by interjecting some comments and suggestions to the peer and to the child, but using language to direct every single interaction and movement is counterproductive. In such a case, you become the director of a stage play, not the facilitator of play.

When you start to use too much language with the peer and you find yourself repeating too many instructions that are interfering with play, consider using flash cards if the peer can read (and your child cannot). Flash cards can say things like "GET ATTENTION" or "SAY 'HELP ME.'" Prompt the peer with the flash card. Other nonverbal prompting mechanisms involve using large posters around the play area and pointing to the appropriate ones during play. You might ask the peer which method he or she prefers or use both.

Also during the briefing, be sure to ask the peer what kind of activity he or she likes to play. Tell the peer about your child's interests and likes and dislikes. Different types of peers will like different activities, so you can prepare your playdates accordingly. You might want to keep notes on your peers to help you remember what sorts of things they like and how they respond to your child. Ask the peer to bring a favorite toy or activity to share with the child.

PLAYDATE STRUCTURE

Once you have located appropriate playdate peers, you should spend some time thinking about the activities that you will have available for each playdate. Plan what reinforcement you will have for both the child and the peer. Although you might have a general schedule of activities for a playdate, it is very important to observe the children throughout the event so that if they are not having fun, you can figure out why and change what you are doing to make the playdate fun. On the other hand, if the children are appropriately enjoying themselves, do not stop them just because you want to complete all of your scheduled activities.

Anything that is spontaneous, interactive, or creative done by either child should be reinforced. Try to get the children to talk to each other rather than through you. Fade yourself whenever possible, and more and more start having the children choose the activities and timing.

EARLY PLAYDATES

Early playdates should be short and reinforcing to both the child and the peer. Have activities available both outside and inside. Since early playdates emphasize proximity of the children rather than interaction, make sure that you have toys that both children enjoy, and can play with independently. If your child has a very "cool" toy, be sure to let the peer play with it. Having an activity that is strongly reinforcing to the peer will, by association, make your child more reinforcing to the peer. Ask the peer to bring toys that he or she likes as well so that they can be shared with your child.

A sharp lady in Alabama told me about a technique that she is using that would have been much better for us in our playdates. When starting out with playdates, make playing with your child reinforcing to the peers rather than force the ASD child to go play with the typical peers. In her playdates, she has her shadow aide set up something really cool with the ASD child and then gets the other peers to join in the play. She then fades herself out. A relationship of sorts is being established by getting the peers to join the ASD child in the cool activity. This is preferable to risking tantrums from the ASD child by forcing him to do something he doesn't want to do with the peer. By creating this relationship, the typical peer will then equate fun (not tantrums) with the ASD child, and the ASD child will equate that peer with fun as well. Both children will be more likely to want to join each other in future play.

In these early playdates, the main goal is to have the children stay near each other. Don't try to force interaction between the children prematurely. This proximal parallel play can occur on an outdoor play structure if the children can remain near each other. Taking the children to McDonald's and having them eat lunch together and then play on the restaurant playground is an appropriate option for early playdates.

Free parallel play may be all that your early playdates consist of for some time. Work to gradually lengthen the time the children spend in proximal parallel play, always reinforcing even small attempts to interact.

EVOLVING PLAYDATES

Evolving playdate activities will start to incorporate more structure: Continue with the unstructured play, and begin to introduce activities that require more interactions between the children. Direct adult prompting of the child and peer may be needed to sustain the interactions. Continue to choose activities that your child knows and likes. As you go along, you may try to include some things that your child does not prefer but is able to play so that you can work on flexibility. However, I would not include these nonpreferred activities until later playdates. The overall playdate should always be reinforcing to your child and the peer.

Activities for these evolving playdates may include:

➢ Free play and outdoor play
➢ Toy play indoors and outdoors
➢ Social physical games and preschool games
➢ Simple turn-taking and board games
➢ Dress up and pretend play centers
➢ Manipulatives
➢ Physical play (sand, water, and playdough)
➢ Community trips
➢ Songs and music games
➢ Arts and crafts projects
➢ Passive activities (listening to music/watching videos)
➢ Snack

As you progress with your playdate experience, increase the number and variety of activities available to the children At first you will be more involved in directing the choice of activities, but eventually, the children should be able to choose which activities to play and in what order. The tutor helps keep the turn-taking straight and has some general timing guidelines. For example, the playdate can be divided into planned sections such as free play, pretend play, arts and crafts, snack, and outside play. The children may then decide on the activities in each category.

A visual schedule can help the children with choosing activities. For example, the children can select picture cards of their chosen activities and put then on a Velcro board. As the activities are completed, the card can be taken off of the board or covered up to help the children make a transition to the next activity. Eventually, let the children take turns picking activities from a variety of choices.

The tutor facilitates interactions and helps the children move from one activity to the other. The tutor may use such statements as "Ok, you guys look tired of the trampoline. How about going inside for a game?" Or the tutor may allow the peer or child to suggest the next activity. You should try to end the playdate on a quiet and calm note.

A huge part of our program focuses on play and social skills. We do one or two playdates each week. One general playdate strategy that worked well for my daughter, especially in the beginning, was using gross motor play activities to help develop play and peer social skills. The rules of simple gross motor games are much simpler than more complex or interactive pretend games, so my daughter responded better to them. At first, we made sure to include lots of activities like chase, tag, catch, ring-around-the rosy, playing ring toss, riding bikes, and playing at the park together.

Another strategy that's been really successful has been having my daughter practice play activities with a tutor first. That way, when the playdate rolls around she's already familiar with the structure and the rules of some of the activities. We did this preparation with simple board games, movement to music, doll and toy pretend play, and some crafts.

Some additional activities include: playing with water (outside or in the sink/tub), playing picnic or tea party with real food (if the child is able, he or she can "serve"), finger painting, playing with toy cars on a mat or rug (I just made my own out of poster board with some of my daughter's favorite places on it), playing follow-the-leader, and making simple crafts (this activity also gives the play peer something to take home to his or parents).

I try to look at what typically developing children of the same age as my daughter are playing (besides Nintendo) and plan similar activities that suit my daughter's needs and interests. Right now my daughter's favorite activity is playing dress-up. We have a Polaroid camera and we take two pictures of her and her friend dressed up together; one goes home with the friend and one goes up on my daughter's wall.

Now that my daughter has been doing this for a while we also let her participate in planning the play date— she gets to choose the activities and put them on a picture schedule, plan the snack, and so on.

THE THEME STRUCTURE

Some people have used a theme format for both their playdates and their playgroups. This thematic approach can be lots of fun for the children, but it does tend to make the playdate much more adult-run and organized. Theme formats might be more appropriate for younger children and for special occasion playdates. They also require more extensive preparation time on the part of the adult. I would consider using this technique occasionally or have a theme for the first half of the playdate and then let the children relax some with simple activities toward the end. Or perhaps have a few theme playdates in the beginning of your peer's experience with your child and then move towards less and less of that format. Some ideas for theme-based playdates and playgroups are in Chapter 14.

THE PRESCHOOL STRUCTURE

Another playdate and playgroup structure mimics that of the child's preschool experience. This type of playdate structure can help the child practice skills that he or she might be having trouble with at school, but remember that playdates are to teach *play* with peers (not school behavior, academics, or social skills directly—although this learning certainly might be an indirect effect). Teaching a child to sit still for circle time is not play. If the activity doesn't look like fun, keep it out of your playdate. If your child is going to preschool, he or she will get plenty of practice at this sort of stuff every day at school. If not, you can work on school skills more directly in therapy. Even typical children take a long time to learn how to behave in circle time, so I wouldn't risk doing something aversive with a peer. A better idea for teaching school skills in a play setting is setting up a school as a pretend play center and letting the children act out the various roles including being the teacher. Playing teacher can be lots of fun for a child. Activities to include in a pretend center school can include story time/circle time, songs, snacks, and games.

UNSTRUCTURED PLAYDATES

As you progress with playdates, begin to fade your directions and peer prompting. Start to teach the child in several different locations with different peers. Ultimately, you will just throw your child into a group of kids. Progressively unstructured playdates are very difficult to achieve in practice. You may feel a sense of panic as the comfort of structure disappears. Your child may display inappropriate behaviors or poor social skills. He or she may experience painful social rejection. You will have to restrain yourself from the temptation to intervene for every misstep of the child.

Here is what I observed in my recent less-structured playdates. The boys (my child, his peer, and the peer's younger brother) played about 10 minutes in a parallel fashion in the sandbox. There was general commenting but no real interactive, cooperative stuff. My child then asked the boys to play with the wagon. For the next 35 minutes, it consisted of them repetitively pulling the wagon up the hill, pushing it back down, jumping in it as it was rolling, and intentionally tipping it over at the bottom of the hill.

At one moment, the peer walked away from my child and his younger brother and went to another part of the yard. I resisted the very deep urge to yell at my child to follow his friend. After all, it was the peer who left the group, not my child. After what seemed like incredibly long 3-4 minutes, the peer rejoined my child and his brother. This struck me as terribly funny because if my child had left the group, I would have run over there and immediately prompted him back, or I would have prompted him to yell to the group to come join him. Anyway, I found it difficult just to sit and see what happened versus immediately getting up and prompting my child.

The kind of general targets we have developed during peer play include the language targets of clarification, 3 conversational turns per person, and staying with or joining a conversation on a topic. Nonverbal targets include appropriate eye contact, reading a peer's body language, and displaying appropriate body language. Behavioral targets include reducing stims and self-talk. Playskills targets include having the child lead, having the child follow, and having the child negotiate or share.

Basically, we are not really trying hard to force those targets to happen. We are watching the peer and our child and seeing when these happen and when they fail. When they are failing, we step in with the prompt or we note it and practice it in a session later.

My, what a hard thing to do. It is so different than the peer plays last year where we were planning every moment. I think that I felt like some sort of Playdate Engineer. Unfortunately, our child and his peers are getting older (5-7 years old) and they don't care for our type of play!

Eventually you will have the child participate in play situations that are unstructured and much freer. In these situations, you can simply walk up to a group your child is trying to join and tell the peer(s) something generic like "He doesn't hear very well and can't understand some of the things you are saying. Just try to help him the best you can and let him play with you, OK? Thanks!" Then stand on the periphery shouting instructions to the peers and to your child if necessary. Kids will look at you as if you are an alien, but they are pretty accepting if their play isn't too disrupted.

Remember that you want your child to be perceived as socially competent, so teach your child appropriate ways of initiating interactions as well as appropriate ways to respond to a rejection. Be careful how you teach this, because certain techniques can backfire, for example, telling your child "If you don't answer others when they talk to you, they will think you don't like them, and then they won't be your friend." First, your child might hear only "Blah blah blah." Second, if a peer ignores your child then your child will think the peer doesn't like him or her and get upset. Instead, just show the child ways to persist in starting an interaction, and if the peer doesn't respond after a couple of attempts, teach the child to switch gears and do something else. The child should also be taught to respond to initiations appropriately, either positively or negatively with such informal phrases as "OK, let's play" and "No thanks, I'm going to play this." You want your child to be polite, but you also have to train him or her to survive in peer situations where politeness may be absent.

Chapter 13
Playgroups

- *Playgroup Goals and Alternatives*
- *Playgroup Peers*
- *Playgroup Structure*
- *Playdate/Playgroup Themes*
- *Free Social Play*

PLAYGROUP GOALS AND ALTERNATIVES

Organized playgroups provide an opportunity for a developmentally delayed child to participate in group peer play while still receiving the assistance of an adult. Playgroups with a variety of peers can offer many opportunities for the child to learn and make friends though play. Peers participating in playgroups can be prompted to play with the developmentally delayed child by initiating social interactions, demonstrating play methods to the child, and creating increasingly complex forms of play. Adults participating in the playgroups provide support for these interactions by monitoring the playgroup and offering suggestions or prompting the peers. Ideally, with adult support, the more sophisticated children will assist the less sophisticated players and continually improve the level of group interaction and play among the participants.

Unfortunately, playgroups do have some disadvantages compared to one-on-one playdates. Most importantly, a playgroup can dilute your child's play experience as a result of all the action and commotion going on. Also, the other peers may start to interact among themselves, giving your child less priority in interactions. Finally, the stress of organizing these groups may outweigh the socialization skills you might gain.

Playgroups can also exacerbate one of the common problems of group childhood play: that is, the level of imaginative play reverts to the lowest common denominator of the group. If you watch a group of children play, the child with the least tolerance for flexibility and imagination sets the level of play. If the other children are trying to play out an elaborate war scenario, they will be unable to do so if one child can't follow or participate. The play will then degenerate into the chaos of children's running around hitting each other with swords.

This problem generally means that therapeutic playgroup sessions develop into highly structured experiences, led by an adult, rather than free interactive play between peers. While adult input is necessary to support the developmentally delayed child, excessive adult leadership and intervention may actually reduce the effectiveness of playgroups in teaching your child interactive play by imposing a rigid structure that inhibits peer-to-peer interaction.

Avoid wearing yourself out reinventing the socialization wheel. While theoretically quite beneficial, play-groups are exhausting to run regularly and take a tremendous amount of effort—sometimes with very little payoff. Instead, see if you can get your child into a local YMCA program or other community program that will allow you to send an aide. The aide or tutor can do the very same type of prompting and data taking that you do at home without your having to worry about the other children or organizing the activities yourself. These programs are organized year round to provide the type of interaction that a playgroup can provide. They have social games, free playground play, and arts and crafts. In addition, you can pick and choose the times for attendance and thus have more flexibility. Many community organizations offer pro-grams that are basically playgroups with a little academics thrown in. These include the YMCA, church "mother's day out" groups, summer preschool (usually pretty relaxed and nonacademic), and all sorts of day camps.

With an aide in place, you can facilitate interaction. The aide can spend valuable time working with your child, not trying to discipline and entertain other people's children. You can also find children for one-on-one playdates in these activities, "test driving" them prior to bringing them to your home. You have the opportunity to prepare these other kids for their playdates before they come to your home. If the group doesn't seem to be working to your child's advantage, you can cut your losses early and try something else.

 Many community organizations have accommodations for special needs children, and they may be able to include your child, especially if you send an aide. I would recommend talking directly to the director of the program, explaining exactly your child's needs and what *you* will provide (they like that) in the way of the necessary support. You don't need to give out your child's diagnosis. Just list the reasons he or she needs an aide and explain how you will monitor the progress. If the program director is unfamiliar with shadow aides, offer to have the director meet with you, the aide, and the child prior to the program.

It is probably better to send an aide with your child rather than going yourself. Some programs don't like for a child's mother to attend, as having parents attend can disturb the other children. The aide will behave similarly to a classroom aide, taking notes on what is done during the day, as well as what is useful and what is not (you can also use these observations to plan your home playdates and playgroups). It is impor-tant for the aide to listen and observe the other children (their duration of play and their language in play) so that appropriate goals can be set for your child. Some people have the aides write down verbatim quotes from the kids to see what sort of play language is appropriate for their child. Adults frequently have very bizarre (and hilarious) ideas of what is appropriate kid talk (i.e., "Excuse me, but perhaps you would like to join us in a game of tag?" instead of "Hey, TAG! You're IT!).

I did a "play group" last summer, I called it my own "summer camp" and I totally went ALL OUT *to make it fun and a successful social experience for my then 6-year-old-son. I had two therapists at once working with a total of 5-6 boys. It didn't go as well as I had imagined. It was way too stressful and nowhere near as socially worthy as I had hoped. This summer my son goes to a YMCA summer camp with an aide (one of my ABA therapists) and it is awesome! He is doing so much better and making big gains socially.*

All that being said, some parents will still like to press forward with playgroups at home. Several playgroup plans that I have reviewed are more geared towards teaching a child to learn preschool skills (following a group, generalizing academic skills, transitioning from activity to activity, following group directions, listening during the dreaded circle time) rather than learning playing with peers. You need to keep your goals firmly in mind. If your child has practiced these nonplay skills in therapy one-on-one, you might be better off sending him or her on to preschool with an aide and letting him or her practice those skills there. Then you can concentrate on his or her playskills at home.

PLAYGROUP PEERS

Playgroup peers are chosen using the same criteria as those for playdates, though you can have a wider range of ages, sexes, and developmental levels. If you choose a range of children, however, you will have to plan activities that accommodate a large range of skills. I would not recommend having another special needs child attend your playgroups—you will spend too much time and energy trying to work with the two children. As with playdates, try to make sure that the peers' parents are relaxed about the whole thing—find children who have already participated in group activities away from home such as those at preschool or day camps. When choosing your playgroup peers, make sure that the children are somewhat self-sufficient. You don't want to spend all your time attending to children who can't manage things by themselves.

When you approach parents about having their child participate in the playgroup, do not concentrate on the needs of your child. Instead, talk about their child and stress all of the fun activities that you are going to provide. Remind the parents that this playgroup will give them the opportunity for a break away from childcare. Discuss with the parents their responsibilities. Tell the parents when you want their child dropped off and picked up. Provide your telephone number and ask that the parents call you if their child is not able to attend a session. Stress the importance of these responsibilities to the parent.

To avoid getting stuck with a poor playgroup peer, just run one playgroup session before you announce a weekly schedule. If you schedule six weekly playgroups at the onset and a poor player comes to every one, you will spend too much time working with that child rather than with your own. Invite several children over whom you are familiar with. Screen the kids and then decide whom you are going to invite for the rest of the schedule. As you find new children, invite them over for one of the weekly playgroups. If they work out, great. If not, then don't ask them back. I wouldn't recommend advertising your playgroup for recruitment, i.e., sending out a widely distributed letter saying that your group is going to meet weekly for an entire summer and announcing all the great exciting things you are going to do. The danger is that you may get some "behaviorally challenged" children in your playgroup and you then can't get them out (especially since their mothers are probably relieved to have them away for a few hours)! Just one of these kids will wreck your whole plan, because these problem children will take too much time away from your child. On the other hand, some of these high maintenance kids actually might be fine for one-on-one playdates, so assess their skills; and if these children are appropriate for one-on-one, then put them on the playdate pool list and invite them back for a playdate.

The best playdates we have are when there is just our kid and one, or at most two, other kids. By keeping the group small, you avoid "cliques" from forming, and your tutor will feel a little more in control of the playgroup. With a smaller group, you'll have less "mutiny" - because I've led playgroups where it takes only one horrible idea to be verbalized and the rest of the group follows along. I suggest picking the three most compliant and reliable kids out of your playgroup pool and scheduling those kids on specific days. Use the old "talk to the Mommy" trick, and say, "Oh, Johnny has such a wonderful time with Billy, but when there's so many kids around they don't get to spend enough time together. How about if they have a special day together?"

PLAYGROUP STRUCTURE

You will need at least two adults at your playgroup. These usually turn out to be the mother and an aide or tutor. It is probably best to have the tutor work with your child while you set up the activities and troubleshoot the whole playgroup. It is less obtrusive to have a tutor hovering over the child than having his or her mother do so. I wouldn't recommend letting the other parents stay unless they know your child very well and are familiar with your behavioral techniques. While well meaning, the other parents will tend to socialize with you while you are trying to run the playgroup and thus become more of a distraction than an asset.

Flexibility in scheduling activities is important here. You will need to have plenty of activities available for the children. However, if they are having fun and doing well in an activity, don't cut it short just because you have to get on with the next activity. You will find that your children's attention spans are very limited; if they actually persist in an activity, treasure that experience. Don't discourage it. There will be plenty of times when an activity that you had planned for a half-hour runs only a few minutes. Plan to keep all activities short.

Be sure to change activities if the children are getting out of control. Insist that everyone follow the group and participate at least briefly in each activity. Have a signal system between you and your aide to start a transition. Guide the children to halt their activity and move on to the next. This transition should be easier if you are gauging the length of the activity to their interest rather than your schedule. Schedule your activities to move the children from the outside to inside and back outside. Changing the play area helps smooth the transition.

EXAMPLE PLAYGROUP SCHEDULE

Free Play (15-30 minutes). Set out activities, books, puzzles, and related toys around the playroom. Or have the children play on an outside play structure as long as an adult is supervising and maintaining proximity of the children to one another.
Group Social Games and Gross Motor Activities (15 minutes).
First Group Activity (10-15 minutes). Plan a structured activity such as an art project or group painting.
Clean Up and Snack (15-30 minutes).
Second Group Activity (10-15 minutes). Plan a more open ended and sensory activity such as sand play or playdough.
Outdoor Play (15 minutes).

PLAYDATE/PLAYGROUP THEMES

Another playgroup structure involves organizing activities around a theme. Using a theme can help keep activities organized. While theme-based playgroups can be very entertaining for the children, be sure that the experience will benefit your child overall. A playgroup structure using a pirate theme could include the following activities:

PIRATE THEME PLAYGROUP EXAMPLE

Free Play. Materials for free play can include dress up materials for the children. Provide lots of pirate hats, swords, vests, belts, eye patches, and flags. Encourage them to play pirate on the play structure outside, pretending it is a pirate ship. Have them "walk the plank." Set up some supervised sword fights. Set out pirate books and the Fisher Price Pirate ship and figurines.
Story Time. Use pirate-related stories. You can also do some circle time activities at this point. Sing pirate songs.
Treasure Hunt!
Snack
Decorating Pirate Vests with Craft Supplies
Free Play Outside

More ideas for theme-based playdates and playgroups are described in Chapter 14.

Despite extensive preparation and planning, many of your playdate and playgroup experiences may not go as planned. You might be very disappointed in what happens. Keep your goals firmly in mind at all times. While running your playgroup, ask yourself, "What exactly am I teaching here?" "Is this experience helping my child's language, socialization, and playskills?" and especially "Is there an easier way to do this?"

As an example of how things can go wrong, read the following observations that came from a mom who tried to run a playgroup for her 5-year-old one summer. Her comments have been echoed by those of other moms:

We decided to do something completely insane this summer. I organized a playgroup (parents not required to attend) at my house, twice a week for three hours each time. I have anywhere from 3 to 6 five-year-olds at my house. To do this, I have to overlap my tutors' hours, which costs me more money. Needless to say, I am counting the days until playgroup ends. I work my rear off organizing activities like scavenger hunts and making gluten-free casein-free snacks that regular kids will eat, only to have some days where only one kid shows up and no parent bothers to call to say that his or her child won't be coming. Better yet, the parents convince me to let their child bring the snack and then their child doesn't show! We have encountered some other unexpected problems such as these:

*1. **Many 5-year-old typical kids do not pretend play**. There is very little of this. We have some kids who flat out refuse. We do have one kid who isn't allowed to play Pokemon, Star Wars, Power Rangers, or anything deemed "violent," but even on days he doesn't come, we still have had kids refuse any sort of pretend. On the treasure hunt day, I got out some old fabric and had it designed so the kids could wear pirate hats and belts to hold swords. Well, only my kid would do it. It seems that* *the pretend play will last a few conversational turns and then end. A kid might jump on a swing and say, "Hey! I am Tarzan," but that is pretty much it. It makes me wonder why we are doing all these pretend programs.*

*2. **Some peers do not respond**. At first, we were told that our child didn't have good eye contact. Then we were told that he didn't nonverbally get his peer's attention (tap on the shoulder). I actually have my son on tape saying, "Excuse me Michael. Can we swap?" while tapping this kid on the shoulder! Anyway, here are the problems with this:*

a. The peer is not reinforcing to our child when he or she doesn't respond

b. Our son takes it quite personally that the kid is ignoring him.
I see this as partially our fault. We had started using social stories such as "not walking away when people are talking to you," "listening the first time to people," and "looking at people." Part of our social stories had lines like "When I don't look at people, they will think I don't care" or "When I walk away from people when they talk to me, they will think I don't like them." Well, now when people do the same to him, he thinks the reverse is true—they don't like him.

We went to the pool the other day. A group of older boys were playing with a ball. Our child swam over there, smiled, and said, "Throw it to me!" They didn't even look at him. The second time our child asked for the ball, I went over there. I then told our child that the boys were just being rude and that he needed to find someone else to play with. He was really upset and started shouting, "Why won't you talk to me?" I then ended up spending the next two days role-playing it out. He gets the concept now that he needs to give up, but I just found myself feeling like such a hypocrite. Here I push this kid constantly to be with other children. I push him to play. If he doesn't respond to a child, he is response-costed immediately. Yet, peers do this a lot—including his friends. It isn't just strange kids at pools but kids who actually want to come over and play with our child.

*3. **The attention span of these kids is very limited**. Do others see this? My tutors and I soon learned we had to have more activities than originally planned. I timed them one day. Painting lasted five minutes and this was an activity that was chosen! Blob lasted four. Freeze tag lasted about as long.*

It is just so frustrating!

FREE SOCIAL PLAY

If you have access to cousins, siblings, and other children who know your child from prior exposure, then you can try to set your child up with free and unstructured social play with them. In these circumstances, the children are just instructed to tolerate the child (this type of instruction is especially important when you ask the peers to play with ASD children who are social but clueless). That is, the child likes to be around other children but can't tolerate the interaction for long periods and without strong social skills exhibits inappropriate behavior.

If your child learns by highly repetitive experience, unstructured social play can be very useful to him or her if the children will tolerate the child's presence and know that he or she needs help in understanding what is going on in the play situation.

For relatives, you don't really have to explain too much. For children that have seen your child frequently (for example, at the local pool), you can simply say that the child doesn't understand a lot of things, but that he or she wants to play.

In this situation, both your child and the other kids will need breaks. Your child might have to separate from the group to recover every few minutes. When we first noticed this behavior in my son, we were tempted to make him continue to play with the group. We found out, though, that giving him breaks actually helped: it allowed him to control the situation somewhat and feel more comfortable. He would always come back to the group after a few minutes of "decompression" and his ability to stay with the group slowly increased in this manner, keeping the group play reinforcing for him.

Chapter 14
Playgroup and Playdate Themes

● *Play Theme-Based Activities*
● *Suggested Activities and Materials for Selected Themes*

When organizing a playdate or playgroup using a theme-based structure, pick and choose from the theme-based activities and intersperse them with plenty of regular play activities. After playdates and playgroups, ask the children which activities they particularly enjoyed. Keep a note of favored activities and repeat them in future playdates and playgroups so that the children will be familiar with the activities. A popular activity can be repeated either as a part of a theme or as a non-theme activity. Also note any unpopular activities. Analyze both the popular and unpopular activities to see if they can be modified to more effectively teach the playskills your child needs to learn. If you know the theme ahead of time, ask the children to bring any related books, toys, dolls, figurines, pictures, rubber stamps, song tapes, CDs, or short videos.

Play Theme Examples
➢ Pirates
➢ Vehicles and Construction
➢ Dinosaurs
➢ Commercial Characters
➢ Beach Party
➢ The Farm and Farm Animals
➢ Space and Stars
➢ Kings and Queens
➢ Pretend Town
➢ Trains
➢ Western
➢ Seasonal
➢ Camping and secret hideout
➢ Sports
➢ Superheros

PLAY THEME-BASED ACTIVITIES

Some activities go well with any theme. Think of the many playskills that you have already taught your child and modify them to match the theme. Don't worry about throwing in a non-theme related activity to the schedule. Make sure the kids are able to do some activities that they are familiar with. Familiarity is important for the other children as well as your own. Try to avoid complicated activities in which you must spend a lot of time explaining the rules. For example, most kids can play with playdough, and if you throw in some theme-related figurines, you are set. Example of activities that can be modified to any theme include:

Decorating Theme-Related Objects
Using your craft box (see Chapter 11) supplies, have the children decorate cut-out paper shapes, wooden objects, plain T-shirts, felt play theme dress-up items, or cardboard boxes. Cut out the theme-related shapes prior to the playdate or playgroup session. Use heavy watercolor paper or other stiff painting paper.

Creating Murals
If the children decorate or paint shapes (for example, dinosaur shapes), you can extend this activity by taping up a large piece of butcher or mural paper to a wall. Then paint or draw a simple corresponding scene on the paper and let the children tape their creations onto it, creating a scene. The children can also draw or paint directly onto the mural to fill out the scene. If you have theme-related stickers, you can have those available for children to stick on the scene if they don't want to paint or draw. Prompt language and *in vitro* play during this activity and have the children talk about their creations and what they are doing in the scene.

Playdough
You can use plain, homemade, commercial, and scented playdough. Find a simple clay-modeling book with pictures for the more advanced children to follow. Make up some examples for the children to model from as well. Use small plastic theme figurines in the play as well. Be sure to supply some of the accessories mentioned in Chapter 9.

Finger Painting
Many children enjoy finger painting, particularly with shaving cream. Just squirt out a mound of shaving cream for each kid and put some powdered or liquid paint on it to mix in, and let the kids go wild.

Rubber Stamps
If you can find theme-related rubber stamps or sponge cutouts, you can let the children stamp on heavy paper or on the mural.

Theme-Related Books
Reserve reading books for quiet times during the playdate. Snack-time is a good time. Ask the children to bring their favorite theme-related books. Use the library as a resource for theme-based books and videos rather than buying them.

Egg Hunts
Use your plastic Easter eggs year round. Put small theme-related items in them (stickers, little figurines, gummi candy) and hide them around the yard. Give each child a container, and let the children find the eggs.

Treasure Hunt
This game is described in Chapter 7. You can modify this to a particular theme by changing the nature of the treasure (for example, hunting for treasure as pirates, hunting for moon rocks as astronauts, or hunting for the stolen crown as kings and queens).

Big Cardboard Boxes

Playing with large cardboard boxes is a childhood favorite. The boxes can be made into anything—a train, a spaceship, a car, a maze, a cave, or a secret hideout. Decorate the boxes outdoors as a group project.

> *There are only a small number of things that were huge hits in my playgroup. The absolute best thing was when I raided the back of local stores and brought home huge cardboard boxes. The kids created two things with these: space ships and a "club house." However, they basically did the same thing over and over again (attack the aliens or attack the pirates) by running out, attacking me or a tutor, and running back in the box. This was done rather repetitively.*

Piñatas

These are always fun, but some of the store-bought ones are hard to break. Homemade ones are smaller and can be made a little more delicately. A simple homemade piñata can be made from a paper grocery sack. Stuff the sack firmly with newspaper so that it can be decorated more easily. Let the children decorate the sack using materials from your craft box. When they are finished remove the newspaper and fill the sack with treats and surprises. Fold the top down and staple it shut. Make a small hole under the folded down part and thread a string through it for handing. Have the children take turns swinging at the piñata with a bat until the sack breaks and the treats fly out! Don't use blindfolds for little kids.

Pin the _____ on the _____.

This classic game can be modified to most themes. Although "Pin the Tail on the Donkey" is the classic game, one can also play "Pin the Hat on the Cowboy," "Pin the Sword on the Pirate," or "Pin the Tail on the Dinosaur." Make up a simple drawing and attach it to a wall. Make several cut-outs of the item to be pinned to the drawing. Use double-sided tape to attach the item. Blindfold the playing child, spin him or her and let him or her try to attach the item to the picture. The child who pins the item closest to the target wins.

Seasonal Activities and Holiday Activities

These include singing popular holiday songs and listening to holiday stories. Holiday activities include making New Year's Chinese Lanterns, making Valentines, hunting Easter Eggs, lighting Fourth of July sparklers, making clovers for St. Patrick's Day, carving or decorating pumpkins for Halloween, trick-or-treating, and making Christmas ornaments. Seasonal activities include building a winter snowman, playing in piles of autumn leaves, collecting and pressing spring flowers, flying spring kites, making autumn leaf-collages, and collecting summer fireflies and insects.

Cooking

Cooking activities can be adapted to a theme or left as a stand-alone activity. Decorating baked good with frosting and sprinkles is an activity that can be easily modified. For example, cookies with theme-related shapes may be used. Make up the dough ahead of time and let the children roll it out and cut it with the cookie cutters. After the cookies are baked, the children can decorate them.

SUGGESTED ACTIVITIES AND MATERIALS FOR SELECTED THEMES

Here are some ideas to get you started organizing your theme-based playdate or playgroup. Remember to keep the activities short and simple.

VEHICLES AND CONSTRUCTION

Toys—Matchbox/Hot Wheels miniature cars, car city track, and accessories, construction playset with crane and vehicles, sandbox-sized construction set, drill truck and car, wooden and large cardboard blocks for making roads, Thomas the Tank Engine or Brio trains, tracks, and accessories, playmats or a play table with roads, tracks, and city building designs.

Dress-up—hard hats, aprons, tool belts, gardening gloves, tools.

Crafts—Small building projects for children from Home Depot.

Books and Videos—Thomas the Tank Engine videos, books, and stickers, children's short construction videos, *Machines at Work* by Byron Barton.

"Dirt" Snack—This snack looks like Dirt! Crush a package of chocolate sandwich cookies (Oreo style) using a zip lock bag. Then, make up a package of chocolate pudding and stir in a small container of Cool-Whip. Fill small, clear plastic cups with alternating layers of the pudding and crushed cookies. Top the cups with a layer of crushed cookies. Refrigerate for two hours and decorate with Gummy Worms.

DINOSAURS

Toys—Figurine dinosaurs of various sizes and materials, dinosaur playsets and playmats, Dinosaur puzzles, Dinosaur match game, and Dinosaur books such as the *Ten Little Dinosaurs.*

Crafts—Have the children decorate dinosaur shapes and murals.

Dinosaur Fossils—Mix up some plaster of Paris and pour about 2-3 inches worth into small paper cups. The plaster begins to set right away, so quickly drop one very small 1-2 inch plastic dinosaur into each cup. Push it down into the plaster so that it is totally submerged. Let the plaster set overnight, and in the morning remove the paper cup. Have the children hammer their plaster block so that it will break apart revealing the plastic dinosaur "fossil" and its imprint in the plaster. You can also hide these in a sandbox first for the children to find.

Pretend Paleontologist—Have the children play in the sandbox, using little shovels, brushes, and picks to dig up fossils (little plastic dinosaurs). Dress-up items can include hardhats, flashlights, and utility belts.

POPULAR COMMERCIAL CHARACTERS AND BOOKS

This example shows how you can take a simple story or character and create several activities for a theme-based playdate or playgroup.

Example—*The Very Hungry Caterpillar* by Eric Carle

The Story—Read the book to the children as a storytime activity or show the video. A puppet version of the story is commercially available that you can act out or have the children act out. You can also use a felt board and cutouts to illustrate the story.

Toys—Have the children put together *The Very Hungry Caterpil*lar Puzzle. Show the children how to make bugs and caterpillars with rolls of playdough and pipe cleaners.

Caterpillar Pretend—Do this as a "follow the leader" activity. Crawl around the room making very loud crunching and chewing sounds while pretending to eat everything in sight. Then have the children and adults cover themselves with towels. Everyone then everyone pops out of his or her "cocoon" and flies around like a butterfly. Little kids seem to like this very silly activity.

Decorating Butterfly and Caterpillar Shapes—After the children have finished decorating cut-out butterflies and caterpillars, you can extend the play by having the children fly the butterflies around or have the caterpillars eat everything in sight!

Snack—Offer the various fruits and foods from the book as snacks.

BEACH PARTY!

Water Play—Bathing suits required for these activities! Use the water play activities from Chapter 10. Favorites for group play include bubbles, water pistols, water balloons, and slip and slide. The children can play in the sprinklers and wading pool, throw the beach ball around, dance in the sand to "beach music," and do a freeze dance. Have a fishing game set up for the children to play.

Toys—Use water-related toys including boats, pirate stuff, ocean floor puzzles, shark and fish puppets or stuffed animals.

Books—Use favorites such as *The Rainbow Fish, Just Grandma and Me* and *Spot Goes to the Beach.*

Sandbox Play—Use the sand-play activities in Chapter 10. If you want to make a more contained activity than having several children play in a large sandbox, make up a few smaller sandboxes with large, shallow, under-bed plastic containers and small bags of play sand. Try adding a small plastic box of water at one end of the sand so it simulates a beach area. Also supply a separate bucket or dishpan of a sand and water mixture for use in making sand castles. Provide little animals and figurines for the children to play with. Bury "treasures" or seashells in the sand for the younger children to hide and find. You can do this outside or on a large drop sheet inside.

Snack—Put Gummy fish, worms, and sharks in partially cooled blue jello for an aquarium effect. Be sure to make this in a clear container or in small, clear plastic cups for individual servings. The gummy fish, sharks, and worms can be served as just a snack themselves.

Decorating Ocean Shapes and Murals—Finger painting is always popular. Consider using blue and yellow paint so that the children can mix them into "sea" green. You can also do finger-painting with shaving cream and powdered tempera paint for a "sea foam" effect. This activity is really messy, so be prepared.

THE FARM AND FARM ANIMALS

Games—Play "Animal Charades" or "Pin the Tail on the Donkey."

Books—Many farm- and animal-related books are available. This is a good theme to ask the peers to bring some materials.

Songs—"Farmer in the Dell" and "Old MacDonald" are favorites with children.

Field Trips—Take the children to the zoo, especially if your zoo has a petting area.

Toys—Toy Farms, farm animal figurines, Spin and Speak for animal sounds, animal puzzles, playdough animals.

Snack—Have the children make ice cream if you have an ice cream maker. Have the children decorate their snack with sprinkles.

Sandbox Play—Use adult or children's outdoor tools. In the sandbox or in a small part of your yard, you can have the kids dig, rake, and "plant" seeds.

Farmer Dress-up—If the children have overalls, have them wear them to the playgroup/playdate. Supply some bandanas and hats.

Felt Board Animals —There is a commercial set for this, but it is small and more appropriate for use by just two or three kids. If you have a large homemade felt board, it will be easier for the children to play with the felt animals.

Crafts—Have the children make some simple animal puppets. For example, have the children glue cotton balls onto a cut-out sheep shape and attach a Popsicle stick to the back. Repeat a similar process for cow, horse, and pig shapes. Those puppets can be painted and have ribbons or strings attached for a tail. Use the puppets to sing "Old MacDonald" and "Farmer in the Dell." The children can also paint wooden animals from the craft store.

Small Pets—If you or your child's peers have small pets available (mice, guinea pigs, small snakes), you can use them in your theme as well. The mice can play in a toy barn in a box. Add some of your little farm animals and watch them.

SPACE AND ASTRONAUTS

Spaceship—Save any huge cardboard boxes you can find. Have the kids decorate them. Then the children can crawl into the boxes and pretend to fly to space. You can cut some holes in the sides to simulate portholes.

Toys—There are lots of space-related toys available including commercial characters and their vehicles (Buzz Lightyear, Star Wars, and Power Rangers). Mix these in with your Duplos and wooden blocks so the children can make their own spaceships and starports.

Dress-up and Pretend—Make astronaut helmets from paper grocery bags. Cut semicircles to fit the bag over the child's shoulders. If you have time, spray paint them white. Then cut a round hole in the front and cover the hole from the inside with *stiff* clear plastic such as a transparency sheet. Don't use plastic wrap or anything stretchy (much too dangerous for children). Then have the children decorate them and wear them to be astronauts. Little flags are fun for them to plant on "Mars" or wherever they pretend to go.

Light Saber Fighting—Use commercial light sabers or, better yet, if you know how to make balloon sabers, make up some of those for the kids to hit with. No one can get accidentally hurt with these. Make sure the kids are developmentally ready to play with balloons (no mouthing!).

Books and Tapes—Use any sort of commercial book or tape that has a space theme. I wouldn't recommend watching a full-length video during a playdate, but you can watch a short appropriate one for a break.

Snack—Try Moon Pies or Star shaped cookies.

KINGS AND QUEENS

Crowns—Cut yellow felt to make crowns. Cut out a large, long, rectangle, and then cut the little points on the top. You can make a practice pattern with paper prior to cutting the felt. Use iron on Velcro to make a closure. Make enough crowns for all the kids. You can put the Velcro on in such a way as to allow some flexibility in sizing or you can wait to size the crowns until the kids show up and iron the Velcro on then. Have the kids wear their crowns during the playgroup. Towards the end, have them decorate them (use fabric paint, sequins, and craft jewels) and take them home to dry. These last a long time.

Dress-up and Royal Parade—Ask the kids and their parents to bring anything usable for dress-up. Collect old jewelry and some old, simple dresses for the girls. Use bathrobes and old suit jackets for the boys. Let the kids wear their crowns. If you have some fancy boxes and little pillows, you can have the "crown jewels" carried in your parade. Sticks and parts of swords can be used as scepters. If you have any sort of knight costume, let some of the kids dress up as knights and carry their swords and shields to protect the royalty. Then have your Royal Parade! Parade out to your play set or somewhere where you have set up some thrones. Let the King and Queen sit and have everyone kneel to them (adults too). If you have any music (Handel's *Water Music* works) play it. You can repeat this little scene until everyone has had a turn at being King or Queen.

Toys—You can use the Fisher Price castle and figures or a similar playset. If you have previously made a castle out of a cardboard box, you can use that as well. Set up scenes using your blocks and Duplos along with the castle. Use swords and shields—both homemade and commercial—for sword fights. Sock-em Bopem makes swords and shields that are soft and safe for sword fighting.

Games—"London Bridge" is fun and simple to play.

PRETEND TOWN

For a one-on-one playdate, you might want to set up just one pretend play center, but for a playgroup, set up as many pretend play centers as you have props and room for. Find all the appropriate dress-up stuff and supplies and set them out. Include a restaurant, a school, a store (any kind), and possibly a fire station. You can have one of the pretend centers catch on fire! Let the kids move from center to center to try out the different roles.

Books and Videos—Anything by Richard Scarry. His *Best Busy People Ever* video is good for introducing community workers. So are his Busytown books.

Toys—If you have a playmat with a town on it, set it up with little people and cars, a parking garage, or toy gas stations. However, in a playdate or playgroup, using the pretend town theme, most of the play is going to be *in vivo* (dress up and pretend) so the children might be less interested in toys.

Snack—Use your restaurant center for the snack. If you want to have the children cook their own snacks, use a simple muffin or cookie mix. Mixing and cooking time is short with these mixes and the children can play in the centers while the goodies are cooking. Assign the roles or let the children choose who is going to serve the snack as the waiter.

Community Scavenger Hunt—Have a list of objects for the children to find that you have previously hidden in your pretend play centers. Each item is written on a note card and labeled with a specific child's name. Tell the children that you are the mayor of pretend town and have lost your things! If they can find all the items, they will get a big prize! Give them a bag to collect the items in. Start the game by giving a note card with the first item written on it to a specific child. Read the card with the clue on it, and have the child look for the item in the stated pretend play center. The other children have to wait for their turn to look for an item. Once that item is recovered and delivered to the "mayor," give the next card to the next child until all the items are recovered. Then have them present the bag to you. Take each item out while you heck off the items on your list. Then give the kids a big surprise!

Chapter 15
School-Aged Children

- *Television and Videos*
- *Video Games*
- *Cooking*
- *Other Activities for School-Aged Children*

When children start school full time, their play activities change. They have a lot of scheduled activities that take up great quantities of their time. Recess at school can be considered a play break, but it usually consists of outside games and informal conversations that can be difficult for typical children as well as for our children.

If a child does not have scheduled activities in the afternoon and evening (a rarity these days) or isn't in an after-school program, he or she might spend some time playing with friends or "hanging out" outside prior to coming inside for the night.

Children spend their unstructured time in the evening watching TV, playing on the computer, surfing the internet (yikes!), watching videos, talking on the phone, reading, or playing formal games (card and board) with parents and siblings.

Some people believe that our children are socialized to abandon pretend play prematurely in favor of organized sports and "games with rules." This may be true. It's frustrating to watch an older child (age 8) pick up a Toy Story toy (a spaceship) and immediately get teased by his friends for playing with "baby" toys.

Most kids past about age 7 or so don't do a lot of pretend play. They want to do sports, rollerblading, video games, go places like swimming, Putt Putt, batting cages, etc. They like to squirt each other with those giant squirt guns, too, or throw a Nerf ball or football. At my 11-year-old's birthday party, all the kids wanted to do was play football and eat pizza. At my 9-year-old's, they all played Putt Putt- and, of course, ate pizza! Trampolines are a big deal with this general age group, too (7-13). I think watching a group of typical kids on a playground and seeing how their play changes so rapidly in just one or two years, from playing on the equipment, to wanting to shoot hoops or play more organized sports is an indicator of where kids' play in general is going. When I was young (before Pangea split up) pretend play, doll play, and simple games like hide and go seek were popular for even preteens, but now kids seem to not want to do those things. They want to play organized sports and video games, go on shopping trips, listen to music, go on sports outings, and go skateboarding or rollerblading. They tend to think of pretend play as babyish. My son with autism is 9. I have an almost 12 year old, and a 3 year old, and am just basing this comment on seeing them with their friends.

Here are some activities that might help you as you try to develop playskills in your older child. I have included only a few since my child is still young. At the end, I've offered some suggestions for additional activities for school-aged children.

TELEVISION AND VIDEOS

It may seem strange to consider watching television and videos as a playskill. However, television programs and videos can be used as tools to teach early conversational skills and language concepts. Teaching your child to discuss videos and TV programs allows him or her to practice the art of conversation with highly reinforcing subjects. Popular videos are also widely known to peers, and this shared knowledge enhances the ability for your child to engage in early peer conversation. As children get older, conversation begins to dominate peer play interactions, so they must be prepared to converse on common topics. Videos and television programs can also serve as sources for repetitive exposure to social situations and provide examples of appropriate (and inappropriate) behavior.

To transform the passive activity of watching television or videos into a worthwhile learning experience, you *must* sit with the child and watch with him or her. You can't be off doing something else. If necessary you can get one of your tutors to sit with the child, but make sure the tutor is trained to wring as much out of the experience as possible. I have a small combination VCR/TV set up on my desk next to my computer. My son sits next to me, and we watch programs together. This positioning allows me to watch with my son and run continual conversation and commentary (I know this is teaching him terrible movie theater habits, but so be it). I do allow him to rewind the tape, although I don't encourage it. Rewinding lets the child review the action and conversation of a particular sequence until he or she understands it. Also, the rewinding allows you to recognize and remember all of the various things that you want to discuss in a particular scene. As my son has progressed in his development, he has stopped rewinding videos, however. Don't be afraid to use the pause or rewind buttons yourself in order for the child to understand the programs.

If the child is familiar with a scene, turn off the sound and have the child describe what is happening. Use the child's favorite action sequences. Doing this activity with the sound turned off makes it easier to talk about what is going on without the distraction of dialogue, music, and sound effects. Have the child sequence the scene as a "blow-by-blow" account. Frequently action sequences don't have any dialogue, but have just music. You can leave the music playing at low volume if you prefer. While prompting the child to narrate the action, you can start interjecting comments and questions about such concepts as predicting (what is going to happen, what the characters might do), emotions (how the characters feel, what they are thinking), consequences, and motivation (why the characters are doing what they are doing). Admittedly, these concepts involve sophisticated language, but if your child is motivated to talk about *something he or she likes,* you will go much further in promoting language than if you pick a topic of no interest to the child and then force him or her to talk about it.

Early Action Sequence Narration
Tutor: "What's happening?"
Child: "The shark chases Ariel and Flounder. Oh, no, Flounder's stuck in the hole! Ariel is pushing him. The shark has teeth. The shark is breaking the ship."

Tutor: "I'm scared! How do you feel?"
Child: "I'm scared of the shark!"

Later Action Sequence Narration
Tutor: "What's happening?"
Child: "Darth Maul is fighting Qui-Gon Jinn and Obi-Wan Kenobi. Qui-Gon has a green lightsaber. Obi-Wan has a blue lightsaber."
Tutor: "What does Darth Maul use?"
Child: "He has a double red lightsaber. He's a bad guy. He has a red face."
Tutor: "What's going on now?"
Child: "They're fighting. Oh no, Obi Wan can't fight. Darth Maul's gonna kill Qui-Gon Jinn. Oh no, he killed him. Obi Wan yells 'Nooo!'"
Tutor: "How does Obi Wan feel?"
Child: "He feels sad."
Tutor: "Why does he feel sad?"
Child: "Because he loved him and he died."
Tutor: "Are you sad?"
Child: "Yes.
Tutor: "What is Obi-Wan going to do?"
Child: "He's gonna fight Darth Maul.
Tutor: "What's happening now?"
Child: "Obi-Wan is fighting Darth Maul. He fell in the generator. Darth Maul kicked his lightsaber. He's gonna use Qui-Gon's lightsaber. He's gonna cut Darth Maul in half."

Consider having the tutor face away from the TV set and have the child tell the tutor what is happening on the screen. The tutor might also consider blindfolding him or herself to dramatize that he or she cannot see the screen. This procedure demonstrates to the child that he or she must tell the tutor what is happening or the tutor won't know. This procedure might be effective in teaching the child that since the tutor cannot *see* what is happening, he or she does not *know* what is happening. This concept (that another person might not know what you know) frequently eludes ASD children, and this exercise works on the development of perspective taking. The tutor may also ask questions to clarify the child's statements. These questions are different from those in therapy: in therapy the tutor is constantly asking the child questions to which the tutor knows the answer. Now, the tutor is relying on the child for information. It seems like a subtle difference, but it is not. This exercise teaches the child that people ask questions because they don't know something, not just to quiz the child.

As the child becomes more sophisticated with action-sequence narration, watch with the sound on. Listen to what the characters say, and work with the child on interpreting their words, feelings, and actions using questions such as "What did he mean?," "Why did he say that?," "Why is he laughing?," and "She looks really mad! What made her mad?" In a particular video, if a sequence stimulates the child, use it and discuss every single thing about it. Talk about the action, characters, dialogue, objects, clothes, settings, emotions, motivations, consequences, music, sound effects, and anything else you can think of. It is tempting just to shut off the TV after the zillionth viewing of the shark scene from *The Little Mermaid* or the generator fight scene from *The Phantom Menace,* but if you really watch each of these sequences carefully, you can teach many things about every second of the action. You can change the interaction of your child with the video from a passive to an active learning experience.

Point out and question the child about characteristics of the video beyond the action and dialogue, such as the music, the scenery, and the setting. For example, I taught my child to listen for musical themes in movies ("Listen! That's Darth Vader's music!"), and he was able to identify musical themes across the whole *Star Wars* series. Talk about the props and objects used by the characters. Point out if they are they same as or different from the objects the child uses: "He has a bike just like yours." "Does that car look like mine?" Have the child identify actions of the characters that are the same or different from his own: "Hey, Arthur has to take out the trash just like you!" Common family events such as vacation and holiday celebrations should be explored and compared to the child's experiences: "Little Critter is camping and is sleeping in a tent. Did you sleep in a tent when you went camping?"

Start explaining why people and animals behave the way they are behaving. Have the child try to figure out the reason for a character's behavior. Work on both the practical reasons for the behavior (to get something done) and the emotional reasons for the behavior (to demonstrate an emotion). See if your child can explain some of the actions: "Why is she pushing Flounder through the hole?" "Why is the Titanium Power Ranger fighting the cobra?" "Why did Pinocchio light a fire inside the whale?" "Why are they dancing and singing?" "Why is she laughing?"

Ask your child to predict what will happen next. Start with sequences that he or she already knows, and then progress to unknown sequences. Have the child predict the actions of the characters ("Now what is he going to do?"), actions of inanimate objects ("Is that tower going to fall down?"), the emotions of the characters ("How is she going to feel when she sees her dog?"). Compare these predictions to the child's life: "What would you do?" "What would your teacher do if you tried to do that?" "How would you feel?" Begin to introduce the concept of reality versus fantasy. Ask the child: "Can this really happen?" "Can dinosaurs really talk?" The difference between reality and fantasy is a tough concept, especially for little kids, so go slowly.

Have the child tell you how he or she feels while watching a sequence: "I'm scared!" Tell the child how you feel as you are watching: "I'm scared too." Progress to having the child describe the characters' feelings: "Thomas is mad." And then ask the child to figure out why the characters are feeling the way they do: "Why is Thomas mad?" "Because the coal fall on him. He's all dirty."

Use videos to begin teaching the concept of humor. If something makes your child laugh, explain that the event is funny and that funny things make you laugh. Laugh with your child and talk about why things are funny: "That's so silly, it makes me laugh!" Be prepared for pretty primitive humor such as people doing silly things with their bodies or the typical "gross-out" humor of little kids. Wait until your child is very advanced to introduce "kidding," riddles, puns, and jokes. Start with the easy stuff like pratfalls and "pie in the face" humor. The subtle stuff comes much later.

While watching videos, begin to work on the concept of good and bad behaviors. Begin with labeling an entire person as a "good guy" or a "bad guy." Much later you can start working on the concept of various good and bad traits co-existing within the same person, but this concept is extremely advanced. Talk about why the person is a "bad guy": "Darth Maul is a bad guy. He's mean and wants to kill the Jedi." Talk about why the person is a "good guy": "Buzz Lightyear is a good guy; he's going to rescue Cowboy Woody."

Later, you can start working on specific examples of good and bad behavior. Start with simple single actions of a character doing something wrong, for example, Sebulba's breaking Annakin's pod racer in *The Phantom Menace*. Talk about why that action is bad (hurting other people's things and cheating), what the consequences are (Annakin's pod racer broke in the middle of the race and he almost crashed), and why a person should not do break other things and cheat.

Once the child is comfortable talking about a video while it is playing, begin to talk about the events of the child's other videos that are *not* playing. If the child enjoys a video series with several episodes, talk about another episode than the one the child is viewing. For example, while watching a *Thomas the Tank Engine* video, mention an event from another episode: "Remember when James ran off the track? How did they get him back on the track?" Talk about the movie or sequence you are going to watch while you are getting the tape or finding the program: "Let's watch *The Little Mermaid*. "What did the seagull do with Ariel's fork? What did he call it? Wasn't that silly?"

All of these narrations, questions, commentary, and discussions performed while the video is playing help the child *remember* the story for later retelling. Try to get your child to retell a sequence that you have previously watched together, by using such prompts as "What happened? Then what happened?" For a long time, your child will not be able retell an entire story without the video playing. In the beginning, you should concentrate on having the child retell a single scene—five minutes long at the most. As you progress, you might be able to get longer and longer story lines and interpretations from your child, and eventually, he or she might be able to summarize a short story (i.e., a single Thomas the Tank Engine episode—usually about 10 minutes long).

Begin to have conversations and discussions about the videos while they are not playing. For example, discuss the shark sequence from *The Little Mermaid*: "Let's talk about Ariel and the shark. Why did Flounder get stuck in the hole?" This repetition helps the child not only remember and retell sequences, but also to learn early conversation skills. These mini-conversations might be repeated many times before your child is comfortable making several conversational exchanges about a topic. Prompt the child to start asking you questions about the video. Obviously our children tend get stuck on certain topics, and such perseveration can be a problem. I must have discussed the color of the various Jedi Knights' lightsabers a thousand times with my child. It was repetitive and ultimately irritating, but *he* initiated the conversations, and I worked hard to get him to say more about each character each time he brought the topic up. Finally, he moved on to other topics. He needed the conversational practice, though, on a topic that was of interest to him and that he knew well.

Finally, have your child describe what parts of a particular video he or she enjoys and why. Have your child tell you his or her favorite characters and what he or she likes about them. Create conversations relating your personal opinions and teach the child to relate his or her opinion about the video. Very importantly, teach the child to question others about their opinions:

Personal Opinion Conversation
Child: "*Jurassic Park* dinosaurs don't talk; the *Dinosaur* movie dinosaurs talked."
Tutor: "Can dinosaurs really talk or was that just pretend?"
Child: "Just pretend."

Tutor: "Did you like *Jurassic Park*?"
Child: "Yes."
Tutor: "Ask me if I liked it."
Child: "Did you like it?"
Tutor: "Yes, I did. I liked the scene with the Velocirapters in the kitchen. That was SCARY."
Child: "No, I don't like that."
Tutor: "Well, what part did you like?"
Child: "The sick Triceratops. Remember he was sick?"
Tutor: "Yes, that made me sad."

These practice conversations can then be transferred to peer conversation. Personal opinions are used commonly for conversation with peers. For example, an early conversation with a *prepared* peer:

Peer: "Did you like *Star Wars*?"
Child: "Yea. I liked Darth Maul and Obi Wan Kenobi and Qui Gon Jinn fighting. Obi Wan Kenobi goes 'Noooo.'"
Peer: "Yeah, I liked it OK. I liked *X-Men* better. That was cool."
Child: "No." (the child is not familiar with the movie)
Peer: "You haven't seen it? I wanna be a mutant and have knives in my hands...like THIS!"
Child: "We have to wait for Episode 2."
Peer: "...uh, Star Wars? Oh yeah, it's coming out next year. I have *X-Men*, you wanna see it, you'll like it."
Child: "OK"

Eventually, the child can be taught to ask reciprocal questions of the peer and thus have a more normal conversation.

Peer: "Hey, you have *Phantom Menace* here, I wanna watch it."
Child: "I really like it. Do you like it?"
Peer: "Well yeah, *duh*."
Child: "OK, I wanna see Episode 2, too"
Peer: "Yeah, me too, but its not out until next year."

We used the movies, books, and videos that my daughter scripted (repeating phrases by rote) as an indication that she was interested in those topics. We used these topics as springboards to conversation. For example, we might say, "Oh, you're thinking about _____. Let's talk about _____." We would then ask questions (sneaking in some of our language goals), and then we would talk about the movie or the book ourselves. We heavily reinforced her for using her own words to talk about her favorite movies or songs. We thought this was really risky at first because we did not want to reinforce the scripting, but it really paid off because (as we guessed), the topics were reinforcing by themselves. We began to get some GREAT spontaneous conversations.

VIDEO GAMES

Video games can range from simple racing games to highly complex role-playing games that involve sophisticated problem-solving skills used during a long storyline. Multiple side stories may also be involved. For several months, my son and I played a Nintendo game called Zelda—The Ocarina of Time, which included elements of puzzles, problem solving, sequencing, playing songs on an instrument, and action. The main character had to learn many physical maneuvers, find and earn money, buy items from stores, help the other characters solve problems, fight monsters, and, of course, save the world. I read the conversations on the screen for my son and played some of the physically difficult parts for him. My child was thrilled with being in control. He could make the character run, roll, ride a horse, swim, dive, flip, fight, and talk. Some of the concepts that I taught my son while playing this game were time concepts, money concepts, trading, sequencing, problem solving, the concept of frustration (when we couldn't accomplish a particular maneuver after several attempts), timing, racing, consequences, the concept of "wasting" (for example, using up all your magic when you don't need to and then not having it when you need it), map-reading skills, sharing, turn-taking, "good guys and bad guys" receiving and giving directions, helping other people, deceit, and using the correct tool for the job. As with television or watching videos, unless an adult is with the child, the activity degenerates into a mindless one, but with direction, it can promote understanding of many concepts and language.

COOKING

I realized that my son was interested in cooking the day I smelled something burning and discovered a "creation" in the oven. My son had poured flour and water in a pan and put it in the oven to bake. Since he had figured out how to turn on the oven and the basics of baking, I figured that I would start cooking with him. Of course, his greatest motivation was eating his creations!

Consider starting very simply with food that requires only a few steps to make. Also make sure the child likes whatever it is that you are cooking. I know people who are purists who want to teach their children to cook only healthy foods (the definition of which varies widely) from scratch and so forth, but I don't think this choice is very reinforcing to the child. I know our children can have dietary limitations, and this limitation makes cooking most sugary junk problematic. If your child is allowed an occasional treat, then make the rule that if the child wants junk, he or she has to make it. Also you can limit junk food eating by baking only small portions. I also have been known to throw away entire cakes after the children eat their first slice. Don't limit yourself to treats and junk though. Try to get the child to cook part of a meal that he or she likes to eat.

I found that backward chaining a cooking activity usually works best. That is, start with having children help at the end of cooking (for example, decorating a cake or flipping a pancake), and then work slowly towards the beginning of the activity. The reinforcement comes earlier this way, and the children can watch you do the early parts and know when to jump in for their contribution. Many people start cooking activities with their children by showing them nonheated activities like making lemonade, pouring cereal, or making sandwiches. I personally didn't do this, because as I felt it was important to teach oven and stove safety immediately after my child's first experiment.

Make sure your child has a sturdy step stool to stand on. My child is tall, but having to reach up to the counter is frustrating for anyone. I also let him dress up for the activity. I bought him a chef's hat at a cooking store and he had a white coat that he liked to wear while we were cooking. He pretended he was a baker or a chef, and this process was very entertaining for him. It also made the activity a mix between pretend play and reality. If you get really energetic, you can set up a bakery or restaurant and do a pretend play center with the food you make. Cooking is also a great playdate activity for older kids. I was surprised when my older child's friends (ages 8-9) gathered around my younger child and me while we were cooking and asked to use the mixer. They, of course, stayed for the cookies that followed.

COOKING ACTIVITIES

Washing hands. Try to remember to have your child wash his or her hands before cooking. This is a good habit, and if you start it first, it might just sink in. If your child likes to get dressed for cooking by putting on an apron or a chef's hat, then incorporate the hand-washing into the dress-up ritual.

Handling Food While It Is Cooking. One of the first cooking activities I did with my children was showing them how to flip pancakes with a spatula. I made the batter and poured it, using a small electric skillet away from the stove. Both of my children got tiny little burns on their fingers early in this activity and thereafter treated any sort of cooking with great respect. Neither of them ever got burned again, and they stayed clear of any sort of touching the stove or oven while cooking. I also had them take grilled cheese sandwiches out of the skillet with a spatula. Stirring food during a stir-fry is also a good activity. You have to show the child how to do this without getting burned or splattering food all over the stove. Stirring stew or soup isn't nearly as entertaining as stir-fry, but it does teach the child how to stir without making a mess.

Cooking in Water. This includes activities like boiling pasta and steaming vegetables. Again, start at the end, and progress forward. Wait until the water is boiling and then ask the child to put the pasta in, as you demonstrate how to avoid the steam. Show the child how to set the timer and then how to drain the pasta. You will need to drain and rinse the pasta for a long time because it is too dangerous for little hands to do. My kid loves pasta, so this experience was very reinforcing to him. As you go along with this activity, you can work towards having the child put the water on to boil and waiting for it to boil. Steaming veggies works the same way. I would not start with having the child prepare the veggies and boil the water. This takes too long and is not reinforcing. Rather, get the veggies ready yourself (I use frozen veggies anyway), and get the water boiling. Show the child how the veggies go in the steamer, and let him or her put them in. Finally, you can show the child how to turn on the stove, but I would wait until very late in teaching cooking to do this!

Mixes, Mixes, Mixes. At this point, I would introduce mixes. I would use boxed mixes that require only a few ingredients. Show the child how to get out the things you need. Frequently there are pictures on the box that you can show him or her, and these give the child visual cues as to what ingredients are needed. Point these out to your child so he or she begins to understand that you are following directions in order to cook the mix.

Next, measure and mix the ingredients. The best tip I ever got for cooking with children was the use of a "slop" bowl. Kids' fine motor skills are not great, and if you try to get children to pour an ingredient into a measuring cup or spoon, they will frequently over-pour and destroy your batter. Instead, have the children measure the ingredients over a "slop" bowl. Then, when the measuring cup is appropriately filled, have the child put it into the real mix that is in a separate bowl. This precaution will keep your good mix from getting messed up from a poor measurement. I wouldn't spend a lot of time teaching your child the fine points of the different measuring devices. This detail is boring, and eventually your child will learn what a teaspoon versus a tablespoon is. Right now you are just trying to show him or her that you do find the correct ingredients, measure things out, follow some directions, and mix them up together to make your creation.

With your first simple mixes, get out your supplies, have the child help you gather up the ingredients, and have the child measure the appropriate amounts. These ingredients might be only the mix, water, and an egg, but that's fine. We are just showing the child how to make a mix of ingredients, not the fine points of cooking. Let the child mix the ingredients using a spoon, whisk, or hand mixer. My child really liked to use the hand mixer, but he usually tired out before the mix was completely mixed, so I just finished it myself. You will usually need to put cake batter in the baking pan, but children can put cookie dough on a cookie sheet. Put the creation into the oven, and have the child watch you set the timer. Call the child back to the kitchen when the timer goes off (if he or she isn't staring at the oven waiting for the goodies), and demonstrate how the hot pan is removed safely from the oven with oven mitts and placed on trivets.

After you remove the creation and let it cool, let the children decorate it. Don't get too compulsive about appearances: most children will tear up a cake trying to get it frosted while it is still warm. Don't worry about it. I usually didn't even remove the cake from the baking pan. I just got out the frosting and the sprinkles and let the kids loose.

OTHER ACTIVITIES FOR SCHOOL-AGED CHILDREN

These include several activities I have not done extensively with my own children, so I don't have the experience to give much direction. I list them so that you can get an idea of some of the activities that your child can participate in as he or she becomes older.

➤ Card games and advanced board games
➤ Sports
➤ Trading cards and role-playing games
➤ Music and musical instruments
➤ Sewing
➤ Martial arts and gymnastics
➤ Gardening
➤ Carpentry
➤ Photography

Bibliography

Bergen, D. and Oden, S. (1988). Designing play environments for elementary-age children.
    In D. Bergen (Ed.), *Play as a medium for learning and development*. Portsmouth, New Hampshire:
    Heinemann Books, 245-269.

DeFeo, A., Grimm, D., and Paige, P. (1988). Talking and Television. [n.p.]:
    Communication Skill Builders, Inc.

Frost, L. and Bondy, A. (1994). *PECS - The Picture Exchange Communication System*.
    Pyramid Educational Consultants, Inc.

Garvey, C. (1977). *Play*. Cambridge, MA: Harvard University Press.

Horn, S., Morgan, G., and Yablonsky, K. (1999). Presentations at a pre-conference workshop as part of
    Innovative and Effective Interventions for Autism Conference, sponsored by Families for Early
    Autism Treatment of Oregon. (January 28, 1999).

Lovaas, O. (1981). *Teaching developmentally disabled children: The me book*. Pro-Ed.

Nyberg, J. *Just pretend!: Creating Dramatic Play Centers with Young Children*.
    Glenview, IL: Good Year Books, 1994.

Partington, J., and Sundberg, M. (1998). *The Assessment of Basic Language and Learning Skills: The
    ABLLS Protocol*. Pleasant Hill, CA: Behavior Analysts, Inc.

Piaget, J. (1962). *Play, Dreams, and Imitation in Childhood*. New York: Norton.

Rubin, K., Fein, G. and Vandenberg, B. (1983). Play. In E. M. Hetherington (Ed.), *Handbook of Child
    Psychology: Socialization, Personality, and Social Development*. New York: John Wiley & Sons.

Smith, M. J. Teaching Playskills to Children with Autism, http://melindsmith.home.mindspring.com

Vygotsky, L. S. (1978). *Mind in Society: The Development of Higher Psychological Processes*.
    Cambridge, MA: Harvard University Press.

Westby, C. E. (1991). A scale for assessing children's pretend play. In Schaefer, Fitlin, & Sangrund (Ed.),
    Play diagnosis and assessment. New York: Wiley & Sons.

Wolfberg, P., and Schuler, A, et al. (1992). *Integrated play groups: Resource Manual*.
    San Francisco: San Francisco State University
    Department of Special Education.

Companies and Products

Bandai America
> Digimon, Akiyoshi Hongo, Toei Animation, Fox Kids
> Power Rangers, Saban Entertainment, Fox Kids

Binney & Smith
> Crayola
> Crayola Dough
> Crayola Model Magic
> Silly Putty

Briarpatch
> Maisy Games based on the chararcter by Lucy Cousins
> Maisy's Color Game
> Maisy's Counting Game
> Maisy's Memory Game
> Original Maisy Game

BRIO Corporation
> Brio Trains
> Richard Scarry's BUSYTOWN

Fisher Price Inc., a division of Mattel, Inc.
> Barnyard Bingo
> Get Better Bear
> Fisher Price Great Adventure Magic Castle
> Fisher Price Great Adventure Pirate Ship
> Fisher Price Great Adventure Western Town
> Fisher Price Robin Hood's Forest
> Little People Animal Sounds Farm
> Little People Main Street

Hasbro, Inc.
> Arthur's Playset from the work of Marc Brown
> Barney, Lyons Group
> Batman, DC Comics
> Candy Land
> Chutes and Ladders
> Connect Four
> Don't Break the Ice

G.I. Joe
Hands Down
Hi! Ho! Cherry-O!
Hungry Hippos
Junior Yahtzee
Jurassic Park, Universal Studios and Amblin Entertainment, Inc.
Lite Brite
Lucky Ducks
Mr. Potato Head
Nerf
Original Memory Game
Play-Doh
Penguin Shuffle
Playskool
Pokemon, Nintendo of America
Splat
Star Wars, Lucas Films
Superman, DC Comics
Tiger Electronics
Tinkertoy
Tonka
Twister
Winnie the Pooh Memory Game

JAKKS Pacific, Inc.
WWF Figurines, World Wrestling Federation Entertainment

James Industries, Inc.
K'NEX
Lincoln Logs
Slinky

Learning Curve International, Inc.
Thomas & Friends, Britt-Allcroft, based on the Railway Series by the Rev. W. Awdry

The LEGO Group
Duplo
Lego
Lego Artic
Lego Champion Challenge
Lego Knight's Kingdom
Lego Life on Mars
Lego Racers
Lego Star Wars, Lucas Films
Lego Studios

Lego Studios, Jurassic Park
Lego Technic
Lego T Rex Transit

Mattel, Inc.
    Barbie
    Hot Wheels
    Matchbox
    Sesame Street, Jim Henson Company, Sesame Street Workshop
    Uno
    View-Master

The Ohio Art Company
    Etch-A-Sketch

Schylling Associates
    MagiCloth Theatre

Tomy Corporation Playthings, Inc.
    Gear Factory

Trend Enterprises
    Dinosaur Match

University Games
    Colorforms

Viacom International
    Blue's Clues, Nickelodeon Jr.
    GAK, Nickelodeon Jr.
    Slime, Nickelodeon Jr.

BOOKS

    Dr. Seuss Stories by Dr. Seuss Enterprises
    Just Grandma and Me, Little Critter Stories by Mercer Mayer
    Just Me and My Dad, Little Critter Stories by Mercer Mayer
    Machines at Work by Byron Barton
    The Rainbow Fish by Marcus Pfister
    Richard Scarry's BusyTown by Richard Scarry.
    Richard Scarry's Best Busy People by Richard Scarry
    Spot Goes to the Beach by Eric Hill
    Ten Little Dinosaurs by Pattie Schnetzler, Illustrations by Jim Harris.
    Thomas the Tank Engine based on the Railway Series by The Rev. W. Awdry
    The Very Hungry Caterpillar by Eric Carle